INTELLIGENT
LEVERAGE

INTELLIGENT LEVERAGE

The **Simple System** That Successful Investors Use to Create Wealth

PAUL HUGGINS

WILEY

First published in 2024 by John Wiley & Sons Australia, Ltd
Level 4, 600 Bourke St, Melbourne, Victoria 3000, Australia

Typeset in Liberation Serif Regular 12.5pt/16.5pt

© John Wiley & Sons Australia, Ltd 2024

The moral rights of the author have been asserted

ISBN: 978-1-394-22129-5

A catalogue record for this book is available from the National Library of Australia

Cover design by Wiley
Cover Image: © Nina/Adobe Stock Photos

Printed and bound by CPI Group (UK) Ltd, Croydon, CR0 4YY
C9781394221295_200324

Disclaimer

This book is dedicated to my wonderful family and the endless number of people who have influenced me over the years, especially those who encouraged me to set exceptionally high standards. It is also dedicated to you, the reader, and all the people who want to get more out of the financial rat race and enjoy this holiday on earth called life.

CONTENTS

ABOUT THE AUTHOR

Paul Huggins is a natural-born entrepreneur, starting as a 16 year old trading $7 luxury car badges in Melbourne, which earned him enough money to put a deposit on his first house before he had his car licence. Today, Paul runs a funds management company called Hamilton-Chase Pty Ltd, which manages over $21 billion globally and is a major investor in commercial, industrial and residential property, and publicly traded and unlisted companies; and Momentum Wealth Management Pty Ltd, an advice and management company wholly owned by Hamilton-Chase Pty Ltd.

Paul thinks deeply about how he manages his time, his health and the choices he makes about where he puts his money. He looks to leverage every opportunity that comes his way, from buying and building companies and acquiring classic cars, to making sure he goes dirt-bike riding on weekends with his teenage son whenever he can. In fact, the inspiration for this book has been to pass on as much knowledge to his son as possible. Every day for Paul starts with exercise and includes some form of meditation.

INTRODUCTION

We all know the biblical quote, 'For the love of money is the root of all evil' and the often-used adage, 'Money can't buy you happiness'. Although these quotes state the obvious, I believe when people say money is not important to them, they are not being truthful—money might not make you happy, but it sure helps.

As this book will explain, since my teenage years I have always had money and I have always been happy. My view is I would rather be crying in a Rolls Royce than smiling in a Mini-Minor.

We all go to school to obtain an education with the aim of landing a career or building a business to make money for the food, shelter and clothing we need to survive. If all goes well, we might aspire to acquire other toys and material things that we all desire—whatever drives or satisfies our impulses or wants at a particular point in time.

Recently, my 18-year-old son commented that I never stop working or thinking about something productive. He went further to say that I always undertake some form of business with almost everyone I meet. I couldn't have put it more succinctly.

That's how I operate in everyday life. While he might have been having a dig at me for being a workaholic, I considered his statement honest and true. My response was, 'What's wrong with that?'

We're all wired differently, but usually only family members are close enough to see your real habits.

The purpose of writing this book was based on a concept I learned many years ago that has fascinated me ever since. It's based on the notion that if I spend my money buying a product or service from someone, what can I sell back to them? This is the general form of trading and has been around since the beginning of time: animals have shared food and shelter for millions of years.

Trade and leverage

I'll admit I trade with just about everyone I come into contact with. This is generally in cash, but not limited to referrals, information, products or a service that I require.

Traditionally, people work for more than 40 years in a vocation of some sort to obtain one income stream from one employer, or run a business they own in one field based at one address. They then become dependent on that one income source and of course spend that income on an endless number of products and services.

Now imagine if the money you spent on products and services allowed you to trade with, say, 25 per cent of those services and receive some form of revenue or some alternative form of payment, ideally cash, in return. It's like the difference between owning an investment property, where you receive some income, or a passive holiday house, where you don't.

I'm always looking to receive income streams from people or service companies where I spend my money, to create a reciprocal arrangement or trade with my products and services.

This can take place in many areas:

- *Property:* buy, own, build, rent and sell
- *Cars:* own, buy and sell
- *Business advice:* share investment opportunities
- *Accounting:* obtain or give advice and referrals
- *Legal services:* obtain or give advice and referrals
- *Networks of people:* obtain or give advice and referrals
- *Social media:* obtain or give advertising and leads
- *Media:* write editorials (which are more credible than advertising) and leads for business or services
- *Seminars:* sell information and networking.

In this era of rising cost of living it's becoming more difficult to stretch one form of income enough to cover the cost of a mortgage, rent, food, petrol, water, power, rates, holidays, health, transport, travel, education, clothing and taxes, just to name a few of the monthly outgoings.

Think about obtaining a reciprocal form of barter such as how you use your time or capital.

For example, after a year of working 70 to 80 hours per week as a property lawyer at Lendlease in the 1990s—earning close to $300 000 per year—I discovered where the real property value was emerging at that time, and it wasn't in the capital cities.

I realised, thanks to my own due diligence, I could purchase affordable homes down the South Gippsland Highway in Victoria's east for around $80 000 to $120 000 each. This was in 1993 when the property market was becoming bullish again so I purchased some of these properties. It wasn't long before a long-term friend of mine called and asked if I would sell any of them. The offers were between 80 and 150 per cent above what I had paid 18 months prior, so I sold three of the properties. I collectively made three times the income I received from working my job at Lendlease for 3360 hours per year (that's 70 hours × 48 weeks after factoring in holiday leave). I worked out I'd spent a mere 12 or so hours of time on the management of these three properties over the same period—and received a much higher return. That was leverage at its finest.

Now, imagine you could sell a service or product in a field outside your full-time job and were paid $4000 twice a month, providing an extra $96 000 per year. Think about how much time that might take—you could probably do it on top of your normal work. Yes, it requires thought and a contact list, but imagine the return compared to your daily vocational income, less tax.

You will never get ahead working at a simple hourly rate of time for money because the deck is stacked against you once you take into account tax treatment, either as an employee or self-employed contractor, and the inability to scale the business beyond what you can achieve with 8 to 10 hours a day of personal exertion.

Bob-a-Job

At the age of 12 I was super excited to join the Boy Scouts. At first, I found it daunting being with guys twice my size, but over time they became very good friends, and I enjoyed the weekends away, building projects and tackling the commando courses. I also thoroughly enjoyed the camaraderie, which was a break away from school, and Scouts offered me a balance in life. It was also the first time I began doing certain jobs for my parents. My father could see the benefits of the additional skills I was learning. I was showing more responsibility, even eventually being able to use power equipment, hydraulic tools and even large industrial jackhammers.

I knew that my desire as a teenager to buy a motorbike (which later morphed into cars), a new stereo system or even the latest in fashion clothing meant I required money. That reality came to me pretty early in life. I would set the alarm for 5.15 am for an early start and looked for ways to fill my day to earn some extra cash.

Most mornings I would head straight to the tool shed in our backyard where I would find myself slinging a paint brush. I would work at jobs such as painting mission brown facial timber beams that extended 30 to 40 feet long for a local builder. I soon added to my skills by learning how to use arc-welding machines, jackhammers and even lathe machines — something that would likely be considered too risky for a child to do these days. I never stopped. One thing I did find out at a very early age is how many jobs I could complete in a day and how much money I could make.

The urge to serve and do more than what I was paid to do is still a motto I live by today that is no doubt driven by both genetic and environmental factors.

There's a term the Scouts used called 'Bob-a-Job'. It means you get paid for completing a job (the money is then donated to the Scouts). Now, this was an interesting time for me as it was probably the first chance I had to create some form of money-making system. My jobs were all recorded on an 8 × 5 index card. For a period of one month (Bob-a-Job month), I would write all my jobs in the columns provided and, importantly, the amount I was paid for each job.

I recall after my first month of Bob-a-Job I ended up raising $11 for the period, which was, at the time, not a record — but from what I understood it was certainly in the top 5 per cent of my group. After that month, I got to thinking, why is this only for one month? How much money would I make over a whole year? So I took the view that I would dedicate myself to the Scout movement for that month every year, but the other 11 months would be dedicated to yours truly.

I created a rudimentary spreadsheet on formatted A4 sheets with my own clientele, being family, friends and neighbours, and it wasn't long before I had getting paid for odd jobs down to a fine art — mainly washing and detailing cars, as well as lawn mowing. A light, electric lawnmower called the Flymo had just arrived on the market. It was perfect for someone still developing physically, like me.

I was also very selective wherever I could be in choosing people who had smaller-than-average lawns, but I still charged them all the same rate. Every weekend I would earn between $45 and $55, which, looking back more than 40 years, wasn't a bad income, with no real expenses. Later I realised that if I could recruit friends to help me clean more cars, purely on the back of demand, I could increase my income. This was my first taste and understanding of leverage.

Through word of mouth and reputation I became very busy and I subsequently recruited my brother and three other teenagers to assist with the increasing demand. They worked for me for approximately 50 per cent of what I was receiving from the customer (family, friends and neighbours). Unknowingly, it was my first sense of what multi-level marketing felt like and how to build scale.

When you're 13, all you want to spend money on is toys. In my case, it was for a serious sound system for my room, which included a brand-new Sansui tuner, Rotel turntable and Marantz tape deck and tuner with 200-watt four-way Cerwin Vega speakers. I think the neighbours in the next suburb could hear my music once I got the system installed. Ferris Bueller's room was amateur compared to what I had in my crib at the age of only 13!

'Fill 'er up mate, and check the oil, water and tyres'

Perfecting my 'Bob-a-Job' car washing and lawn mowing service for friends and local neighbours wasn't enough. I needed more and I needed to lift my game as well as my level of service and knowledge of other services that I could become good at achieving. I contacted the local Caltex service station at the age of 14 to inquire about a part-time job. Even though the age for working was legally 15, I rocked up one Friday evening and presented myself to the proprietors, Barry and Ray — who were good friends with my father. I told them I was ready for the task, irrespective of age, and that I had been around cars, motorbikes, petrol and oil since I was old enough to slide under a car — probably at the age of four or five.

To be honest, I wasn't sure I'd get the job until I received the call that my application had been accepted, admittedly at a very modest hourly rate. I was excited but didn't realise I was given the worst possible shift, being 4 to 8 pm on Friday and Saturday nights. While all my friends were having a great time roller skating, or going to the movies or blue light discos (and probably doing things that I shouldn't have been doing at that age anyway), I was pumping petrol at the Caltex service station on 35-degree days in summer, and what felt like zero temperatures in winter. All the while there was only one uniform: a Khaki green army shirt with a Caltex logo and my name embroidered on the left-hand-side pocket.

After a while, part-time work and school became a routine for me. I would run in the mornings; I would study long and hard and do work for my father; and then I would go to the service station. By the age of 15, with my continuing (largely outsourced) services of washing cars and mowing lawns, as well as keeping up the service-station job, I was pulling in approximately $180 a week—and I was only just legally able to work. To put that into perspective, this was in 1982 when $180 went a long way. I remember filling up assorted biscuit tins with wads of cash and ramming them in so tight that the lids popped open.

I'll admit as a kid I was reluctant to deposit the cash in the bank because I loved the feel, the look and the smell of money. Along the way I never considered the work I did as work, and that made it seem easy. For me, feeling tired after work and ready to go to bed early and sleep well provided a sense of achievement, comfort and security. It was an important habit and routine to pick up at that young age.

There are also opportunities that come with hard work. At the service station, the roster of Friday and Saturday nights didn't concern me at all after a period of time. In fact, it helped me develop a love of high-end classic European cars in particular. That's because we had a lot of doctors, surgeons and accountants in the area who would stop by on their way home or on their way out on Friday or Saturday nights around 6.30 pm, and I took particular interest in knowing how well certain cars were maintained or restored.

It wasn't long before the owners and the customers of the service station realised how much care I took lifting the bonnet, changing the oil or water, checking the transmission or washer levels, cleaning the windows, checking the tyre pressure and, importantly, not filling up the tank too much so it spilled over, which could damage the paint.

There were always three of us servicing cars, but as I became so good at it, certain customers would almost demand that I attend their vehicle, even if I was busy with another car. That meant they would stop and wait until I was ready to help them. These cars were anything from Mercedes 300 SELs (6.9 litre or 6.3 litre), Mercedes SL500s or Porsche 911s or 930s as well as the occasional Ferrari.

They were the cars I remember vividly, involving possibly 25 to 30 clients out of the hundreds that came by the service station over the weeks.

As I got to know these drivers, we'd talk and I learned to network. They would tell me what they did, how they got into their role and their general achievements in life. This gave rise to relationships with people who were between 35 and 40 years older than me. I found it interesting and rewarding that I got to interact with older, more experienced people, from whose wise words I could learn so much. That would never change as I got older.

What a teenage love of luxury cars taught me about leverage

Given my interest in imported European cars, it was probably predesigned that expensive cars would play a significant role in my life. Soon, the penny dropped that I could 'leverage' an opportunity to create serious wealth as a teenager.

I was about 16 (and still working at the service station) and I recall that where I was growing up there were vandals using screwdrivers to take the badges off the bonnets of expensive luxury cars such as Ferraris, BMWs, Mercedes and Porsches to either sell or keep. It was maddening for the owners of those cars because to replace the brand badges cost hundreds of dollars and was a major hassle.

About that time, I was on a holiday in Hong Kong with my grandfather and I noticed a shop selling those same car badges— I assumed they were replica badges—for $7 each. They came boxed up and professionally presented and I was impressed with the quality. As a result, I bought some in Hong Kong and when I came back to Australia I approached a few luxury car clubs to promote the replacement badges to their members. I did some rudimentary advertising and branding and sold them for close to $100 each—about a quarter of the price car owners paid the dealers.

The business took off! By the time I was 19 I was earning close to $18 000 a month in this car badge trading business, while starting a law degree at university. I was even able to put a deposit down on my first home with the money I was making. I couldn't believe my luck: I would put in an order from the supplier in Hong Kong and sell them locally in Melbourne.

One day, just before my 20th birthday, I received a letter from the head office distributor of Ferrari. I've got to say I opened the letter with trepidation. It was a 'cease and desist' legal letter, threatening me with legal action if I didn't stop selling my Ferrari badges. They invited me to a meeting to discuss the matter in person.

I went along to the meeting, and they wanted to know where I had bought the badges. I explained about the shop in Hong Kong, and they asked me to sign a legally binding document, a release deed, that effectively prohibited me from selling them in Australia ever again. I was then asked if I had any more badges. I replied, 'Yes, of course'. I had put them in my car boot because I thought they might want to confiscate them.

On inspection, the Ferrari executives were surprised to see there were hundreds of badges. I explained that I had spent thousands of dollars buying them and did not want to just give them away. The Ferrari team then offered me an undisclosed sum to cover the cost of the products and all my expenses for the badges. I agreed to their offer on the spot. Those funds allowed me to almost pay off my first home mortgage and got me into property investing in the mid 1980s. Eventually, I would also run a property development company as part of my investment corporate structure.

I learned a great deal from that teenage experience. I learned the fundamentals of finding a scarce resource and selling it at a sizeable margin. I discovered the power of networking and marketing as well as the importance of distribution chains, from the supplier to the end consumer. I also learned that you have to leverage an idea and plan a business strategy.

I lived the JFK vision of 'it's not what your country can do for you, it's what you can do for your country', but in my case it was for customers, clients and other people.

In short, I learned the beginnings of what I collectively call 'intelligent leverage'.

From fear to success

With the desire for growth comes fear, but when you take the leap of faith results will follow.

We all have insecurities and to overcome them means changing your brain and resetting your belief system.

On almost every occasion when I am embarking on a project or business venture, borrowing money or have a significant project presented to me, there is an element of fear or doubt.

Public speaking is a common fear we should all try to overcome. The record shows, after 50 years of surveying the Western world, that people will choose to walk over hot coals or pay tax rather than having to speak publicly.

One of the best formulas or remedies for overcoming fears is a careful, deep understanding and gathering of knowledge in your chosen task, project or career.

One of my greatest mentors at Lendlease was CEO Stuart Hornery. Stuart once said to me that if you have a huge amount of responsibility from a young age your peers will resent you and try to come after you because of your title. So, he said, the thing you must do to tackle this is, to know more than anyone else on your subject. That will eradicate your doubt and fear.

Most people, I have found, will bluff or talk their way out, assuming they can sell their wares by assuming entitlement to their position, or enter a negotiation or pitch to get ahead. The reality is most of these pretenders are exposed after a period of time.

Nothing takes the place of expert knowledge and study of your chosen field.

Fast forward to today. After a short career in law (I had to try because my great-grandfather was a Justice of the Supreme Court of Victoria), while I rose to the top as a property lawyer I was never really satisfied with law. This was mainly due to the fact I was selling my time for billable hours at a rate that could not properly leverage my skills.

Stuart Horney provided me with an opportunity to move within the company to manage a $2.4 billion property fund that had halved in value after the post stock–market crash of 1987 and then soon after had become a victim of the early commercial property correction. This meant I moved into funds management.

Stuart had seen my potential well before I recognised it. That opportunity, though I didn't immediately recognise it, changed my life dramatically.

Initially, I learned a great deal working for Lendlease, one of Australia's largest funds management businesses, before starting my company, Hamilton-Chase Pty Ltd, which now manages close to $21 billion of funds for global investors. I have also used the business models of Lendlease, Macquarie Bank, Bridgewater and Associates and Berkshire Hathaway as my Holy Grail of investment thinking.

Lessons I've learned over my working life

We are all a product of our upbringing and the environment in which we live. I had successful role models, including my father, grandfather and great-grandfather, for which I am very grateful.

My father was a great businessman and a serious collector of classic cars; in fact, he loved Jaguar cars. I remember taking his favourite 1951 Jaguar XK120 for a drive (without his permission, of course) to impress a girl when I was a teenager—well before I had a drivers licence.

To this day, in my mind, I still thank the policeman who caught me driving that night, showed me more leniency than I deserved for what I had done and told me to drive home immediately. I learned a big lesson that night: be creative, but don't break the law.

On the upside, I have inherited my father's love of classic cars. I bought my first car (which became a classic), a 1984 BMW 635CSi, for $6100 when I was 18. I did some work on it (and enjoyed driving it as fast as I could for a few years) and then sold it for $18650 when I was 21. Today, I have more than 100 classic cars.

Why? As this book will explain, the right classic cars fit all the criteria for intelligent investing: they are a finite source (you can't build any more classic Porsche 911 cars); they are in constant demand (especially those that became part of popular culture, such as the James Bond–inspired Aston Martin DB5); and they are something you can actually enjoy (try taking a stack of government bonds out for some afternoon fun in the sun).

Wanting to enjoy life with your investments is also an important goal you will learn about when reading this book—and it is a great motivator.

We can't all own an Aston Martin DB5, but we can empower ourselves to do better. We have the tools at our disposal; we just need to leverage them.

The main lessons I have learned along the way are to think about and plan your finances, business, work–life balance and commitment to family carefully. If you don't, your time will be wasted, and your ambitions will fail and break down.

As you will learn in this book, your state of mind is very important for success in any form, as a clear mind will invariably determine your output.

In short, the three most important actions that must take place for the average person are as follows:

1. *Purpose:* a reason for jumping out of bed each day. A list of goals is a great start.

2. *Motion:* motion of the body fires the neurons in the brain. Bodies need to function because the alternative, which is to remain in bed or stagnant, will work against you and invariably sends a message to the brain of a hibernation state. Exercise is critical. I weigh the same at 56 years of age as I did when I competed at professional-level running at the age of 21. My weight at 75 kilograms today has been my weight for over 35 years, and while it gets a little harder with age, a proper diet and embracing certain healthy foods, along with some supplements, helps to maintain my weight.

3. *Gratitude:* if you think you're having a bad day, just stop and take stock, read about others who are less fortune, or talk to people who live on the streets or have a disability—not to pity them, but to understand the beauty of life through their eyes and minds. That will shift your perspective.

We all know a lot of people younger than us who have let their bodies go physically and whose lack of performance has become evident. If you can't take care of your body and mind, how can you be given the responsibility to run a company — or a family, for that matter?

There is little point chasing success if you won't be around to enjoy it with your loved ones.

Many hard-working people's view of exercise would be taking a bath, pulling the plug and fighting the water current as they climb out!

There are plenty of lessons to be learned from this. Set high standards and treat every person like a king or queen. The realisation that every person is important and can dramatically help you in some form is critical.

Don't act too quickly, especially without rational thought, but at the same time don't procrastinate over your decisions. It's only once a decision has been made that you will ever build anything of significance.

We can't achieve everything on our own, which is why I always question the phrase 'self-made success'. We will always need the assistance of other people or access to other resources, either provided by banks, institutions or governments, coupled with the labour and services provided by other people. Your networks and contact lists will always be the most important asset you possess, other than your health, of course.

Always be clear and precise in your communication. The ability to speak, convey clearly and articulate your position is a critical tool in life and in business. Most business relationships, or anything that requires human intervention, can only be stimulated by communication.

If you make a promise, you must always follow through on it. Trust is a commodity that you can't buy, but in my world, it is highly bankable.

Relationships are something we all need to invest in continually. I estimate over the years I've spent more than half a million dollars travelling the world to attend conferences, meet up with business contacts or just network. It means I have had the luxury of meeting astronauts, two serving presidents of the United States (Bill Clinton and Donald Trump) and three Australian prime ministers, as well as business leaders such as Elon Musk, Bill Gates, Warren Buffett, Ray Dalio, James Packer and many more.

I can't tell you what the exact return on that investment would be, but apart from the influence meetings such as those had on my way of thinking, as well as opening up business opportunities from the people I met on those networking trips, it would easily add up to many millions.

As former Liberal leader, Dr John Hewson—with whom I have worked on many successful projects in the past—was keen to say: 'Leaders at all levels must state their claim and be clear on what they stand for'.

I am very grateful when I look back at some of the incredible people I've met through my travels, some of whom have told stories that have inspired and motivated me, and encouraged me to do more and better. The reason I mention this is I've found that the type of people we associate with will either attract success or encourage failure in our lives.

These days, as you'll read in this book, I'm very particular about the people I keep in my inner circle. They must have similar interests or the same mission of working in collaboration in the pursuit of a mutually beneficially project. I am very conscious of time; I don't like wasting time and I try to be high on life as much as I possibly can. My work and personal relationships, partnerships, general beliefs and religious beliefs all fold together into one. I find it hard to separate them. It's the person I've become.

How I live a balanced life

Another significant thing I've learned is to have a balance in life. I have myriad wonderful things happening constantly. I'm not one to relax in a hammock for three weeks on a holiday. Instead, I'm constantly thinking about people, products, services and business. I have found that doing transcendental meditation every morning and afternoon helps me immensely, particularly for generating vision, clarity and understanding as well as the processing of strategies and people.

My daily life consists of going to bed before 10.30 pm, enjoying a deep sleep and waking before 5.30 every morning. I then like to meditate for 20 minutes in the early morning, after which I dive into my pool 365 days a year at around 6 am—no matter how cold it is. During winter, when the temperatures might fall below five degrees in Melbourne in the early morning, I find diving into a cold pool refreshing. It resets my whole-body thermostat and mind. It's like a car getting jump charged.

My morning routine continues with a physical workout four to five days, a week usually consisting of heavy weight training including legs, back, chest and other minor muscle groups. I concentrate on

20 to 30 minutes of aerobic activity at least three times a week. I believe in eating a very high protein diet for muscle retention, strong organic foods and low processed foods, which involves ingredients in their most natural form.

As far as supplements and vitamins go, I take amino acids and myriad multivitamins—sometimes up to 20 tablets a day. I think the hype around drinking one or two litres of water a day is overstated. I tend to concentrate on obtaining six to eight glasses of water a day. My weakness is coffee. I consume at least two cups before I hit the road in the morning. I'm in the office by 7.30 am.

By the time I sit down at my desk on a Monday, I have carefully worked out my full day and what I have to achieve that week. I usually have 20 items in my diary to complete per day with 10 major items or goals that must be completed by Friday at 6 pm, before I leave the office.

I tend to keep alcohol (especially hard spirits) out of my life, although I have a real appreciation of and enjoy champagne. It's not unusual for me to have a glass of champagne three or four times a week.

How I invest in myself

My core beliefs generally are being better and trying to improve myself every week, month and year. I'm constantly focused on what I'm doing in relation to my goals and have a daily routine of visualisation, which is a very, very powerful tool.

In fact, visualisation has been one of the secrets to my success in being able to think deeply about how to achieve a goal. If you live and breathe it, it's more likely to happen, and sometimes you need to even embrace that goal as if it's already happened.

Visualisation, communication, focus, drive, commitment and a deep-seated desire to be successful are elements most people find difficult to maintain constantly. I find these days I'm usually 'on' for 9 to 11 hours a day. I don't have any shallow friends and I am very quick to cut short any business transactions that I don't think will work. Remember, I receive over 300 business proposals a year and probably end up acting on a handful of them.

I'm a big believer today that while most goals are important, people should have fewer goals and set higher standards.

I like to be clear about my goals daily and carry them with me — that's what keeps me high on life. The inspirations in my life growing up have always been the likes of Elvis Presley, who broke through barriers and inspired generations, and Donald Trump in his prime, when he taught the world about the power of communication, creating a brand and the importance of self-belief. I've always loved the dress sense of people such as actor Gregory Peck, packaged together with the charisma and friendly personality of fellow actor Robert Redford.

In an intellectual sense, I've always admired the tenacity and imagination of Albert Einstein and Elon Musk and the work ethic of Jeff Bezos.

Values and integrity are critical and for that reason I think we all admire the vision of John F Kennedy, and the creativeness and insightfulness of Bill Gates and Steve Jobs.

And I can't leave Warren Buffet off this list. He keeps me calm at night when I put my head on my pillow knowing that I must have the patience and perseverance to see through my investment strategy.

You need to reach out and seek out influential and knowledgeable people. This is not just via social media, Facebook or Instagram, nor is it via an email from time to time. It is about taking the necessary steps and channels to spend the time and the money to meet them in person, which is not an expense, but an investment in yourself. Don't waste any time.

***

This information in this book has spent years gestating in my mind. I hope it brings you as much joy reading it as it has brought me to finally capture it all in the one place.

PART I

FUNDAMENTALS OF INTELLIGENT LEVERAGING

CHAPTER 1

LEVERAGE AND POWER: MAKE IT, KEEP IT AND LEVERAGE IT

Leverage comes in many forms, not just the obvious, which is borrowing money against assets. Leveraging correctly is probably the most powerful concept for anyone wanting to succeed in business or in the investment world. Doing it in the most intelligent way means controlling the structure and platform of your asset base and building the right networks and ecosystem to catapult you into the next stratosphere towards financial independence. The knock-on effect and outcomes include the ability to help not just yourself, but others as well.

The good news is that you probably already have most of the tools in your toolbox to achieve this — it's just that most people don't use them or know about them. The famous French visual artist Henri Matisse has been quoted as saying: 'I don't think outside the box. I think of what I can do with the box'.

There are ways to empower yourself to use leverage to achieve yourself goals. It's not about trying to find the next big thing to make you rich, or giving you specific stocks and property to buy, but highlighting what the long-term and future trends in investing tell you about where to put your money.

There is no return on personal investment quite like the return on your own exertion via research, engagement with others and properly managing your time and resources. In short, it's about employing *intelligent leverage*.

There are various types of leverage, including:

- *Financial leverage:* when an individual or small business uses borrowed funds to invest or grow its business. Financial leverage also includes getting the right tax settings, looking for investment opportunities, getting out of the mindset that superannuation will always look after your retirement and getting active when it comes to setting financial goals.

- *Human leverage:* getting the most out of your own skillset by asking yourself, Am I focused enough? Do I know what I want? Do I get enough sleep? Add to that using other people's time, skills and resources to enhance your investments or to grow your business. Getting the right advice is critical, whether it's from a financial planner, research analyst or a mentor who's already been successful in what you're trying to achieve. Networking is also critical to great outcomes.

- *Physical leverage:* being match fit. We all know running a small business or managing your own investments requires putting the time and effort aside for research—and that requires considerable physical and mental commitment. To be successful, you need to be up for the fight, which means keeping fit and alert, managing your time better and setting goals for your own personal life that enhance your financial goals.

- *Informational leverage:* information is king and that means keeping up to date with the trends and issues that can affect your investment goals or the external actions that can affect either your business or the business in which you'd like to invest. This in turn means doing lots of reading and exchanging information with people on the same journey as you. In the future, it will also inevitably mean embracing AI technology. But you must never give up control of the direction in which you want to head, so think of AI just as another helpful tool.

Most people don't know it, and it's scary to think about it, but they are constantly falling behind—especially if you think old age and retirement will look after itself.

However, it is possible to safely focus on acquiring assets you can rely on over the medium and long term that are less risky than what is being offered by the global listed share market. A simple look back at 75 years of asset classes and trends regarding net returns shows this to be true.

The assets that are more reliable and have survived the test of time are property (land and real estate), gold (and other rare metals including now rare earth elements), rare collectables (including art and other asset forms including classic cars and wine) and traditionally different forms of energy. What these assets have in common is a limited amount of supply. You cannot create more land or gold, or an original piece of Picasso artwork.

Then there are other factors that can work in your favour, such as maximising the tax system, which in Australia's case is written in favour of real estate. What's notable about tax is that financial advisors cannot really earn a dollar from buying or selling the family home or an investment property like they can when they recommend other financial products. Yes, the banks get their share when they provide a mortgage, but for these asset classes the individuals receive almost all the upside.

A lot of effort by financial planners goes into trying to limit the tax implications of various forms of investment or business operations, whether it be income tax, payroll tax, fringe benefits tax, stamp duty, goods and services tax (GST) or capital gains tax (CGT). While tax advantages must be factored into any decision making, the more important point is that tax outcomes should not be the sole intention of your investment strategy.

The first type of leverage most people think about is financial leverage and its most obvious use, which is to borrow money to invest. It is this form of leverage that we will focus on in this chapter.

Financial leverage can be used to help purchase your home or an investment property, or to buy shares on the stock market—either in Australia or overseas. Businesses use financial leverage to fund their growth, and individuals apply this form leverage to buy a car or pay off debt. Professional investors—sometimes called day traders—use leverage to boost their investment strategies.

Forms of financial leverage

'Financial leverage' can have various meanings, whether it be for personal investing, achieving personal goals or investing in a business. In an article from *Forbes*, leveraging is described as 'the use of debt to help achieve a financial or business goal'.

Typically, there are four main forms of financial leverage. We'll take a close look at each of them next.

1. Business leverage

Business can be brutal, but at its heart it is an intellectual sport.

Financial leverage is a way to fast-track business growth plans. Businesses use leverage to generate the funds to launch new products, to expand operations, undertake new projects or acquisitions or to simply meet an increase in demand by buying more inventory to be used in production.

When a business decides it will take the option of financial leverage—which could be anything from taking out a loan, to issuing bonds to existing shareholders—there can be many long-lasting benefits compared to selling down equity (by issuing more stock) or taking the option of selling off part of the business to raise funds. Of course, loans must be repaid with interest, and this can create cash-flow issues—but...

One important measure to assess financial leverage is how much debt a company has in relation to the amount of money its shareholders invested in it—known as the debt-to-equity (D/E) ratio. Investors and all other creditors will closely monitor this measure to assess if a company would be able to repay all its debts through the funds it raised. In general terms a comfortable D/E ratio is about 1 to 1.5.

A company with a risky investment profile has a high D/E ratio, unless of course the existing investors have embraced the strategy because they can see the upside of how the additional funds will be invested and how future improved cash flows can finance paying down the higher debt levels.

Small businesses—which don't have the same options as big businesses to access funding —are often reliant on this type of leverage. Start-ups in particular may not have a lot of capital or bank deposits to draw down for available funding. These businesses have several options, from taking out small-business loans, to utilising their business credit cards (watch out for interest on these if you don't pay off your card regularly) to finance their operations.

Just remember, when you take out a loan or a line of credit, the resulting interest payments are tax-deductible, which makes utilising this form of leverage even more attractive.

Of course, taking on too much financial leverage can also be problematic—not only because the loans need to be serviced but also because future investors, when evaluating a company, might be scared off by the company's level of debt or tight cash flow.

Another measure for business that is important to both investors and creditors is operating leverage. This measures a company's ratio of fixed costs to variable costs. There is no right or wrong measure of this equation—it just depends on how a business might operate. For example, companies with high ongoing expenses—such as manufacturing firms, which require a lot of machinery to produce products and have significant fixed costs—have high operating leverage. Potential investors would be asking what would happen to a company with high operating leverages if it were to hit a downturn in sales or were not operating at full capacity—for example, if it had machinery constantly breaking down. In this scenario, with its fixed costs still high, the company would find it more difficult to turn a profit, which would be bad for investors expecting a strong return.

To help most businesses grow or achieve a return for the founder, many businesses list on their relevant stock exchange. That means the founders reduce their share of ownership by offering stock to other investors. This is done via an initial public offering, or IPO. At its heart, an IPO involves selling some form of securities to the public in an open market. For many companies, selling these securities raises much-needed funds. However, they can have an indefinite maturity (unless the company goes private again at a later stage), so selling shares also brings with it responsibilities to shareholders.

Once a company is public, it can sell further shares, spilt shares or use other tools such as issuing options to continue to raise funds in the public capital market. For that reason, an IPO is an important step in the growth of any business.

However, independent research in both Australia and the United States shows most IPOs fail (meaning the company either doesn't last or the shares don't reach the value they listed at)—but of course there are examples of spectacular successes as well. I mean, we all wish we'd bought Apple shares at $US0.10 in December 1997. A Nasdaq analysis of companies that have gone public since the 1980s shows the IPO success rate is about 20 per cent. This means that 80 per cent of companies that go public end up being unsustainable (and most will remain unprofitable) when they make their debut on a stock exchange.

Analysis of the past 60 years shows that 87 per cent of companies listed on the S&P stock exchange have gone bust. Even more worrying, 97 per cent—or 435 companies—of the Fortune 500 list from 1955 are no longer around. We know that some companies—such as Kodak and Pan Am—lost relevance and disappeared into the sunset because they failed to grow or didn't evolve to meet changes in customer behaviour.

Here's something you'll hear me say a few times in this book: the paranoid will survive, and no business is safe. The key to success in business, and all forms of investment, is to be nimble, open minded and have a great dose of paranoia about what your competitors are doing.

Businesses, big or small, must pay close attention to the environment in which they operate. That means seeking professional help where needed to read the environment for shifts in financial markets, changes in government political and tax agendas and likely moves in interest rates, which can dramatically impact your cost of leveraging.

Over time, I have found that the more in tune a company is with its environment on a daily basis, the better its ability to forecast the short to medium term.

The esteemed Albert Einstein, while he worked as a professor at Princeton for nearly 20 years, issued the same questions to his students year after year until, after a few years, some of the students and the Dean of Princeton caught on to what he was doing. Einstein was asked why he posed the same questions every year. His answer was telling: because the answers keep changing.

What does this tell us? Keep asking the same questions because when you're dealing with different issues, the answers will be different.

Most successful business leaders have, at one time or another, used financial leverage. When Andrew 'Twiggy' Forrest at Fortescue had a D/E ratio of about 70/30 per cent to establish his iron-ore project in Western Australia, many investors were nervous and sceptical. At the time, Forrest was determined to push on. He told the *Australian Financial Review* that 'Vision is often derided, but it is lack of vision which is the real failure of a chief executive or a board'. His leveraging worked and he financed his own rail line to take his iron ore to the export market, bypassing competitors such as BHP and Rio Tinto. That is how he generated his megawealth.

On an international scale, the great US business magnate John D Rockefeller (1839–1937) liked to use loans from banks to buy out his competitors in the oil industry, creating a global conglomerate worth billions of dollars. His catchcry was always, 'Make your money work for you'.

Of course, the Rockefeller family today are still huge investors everywhere, even in Australia. I had my own personal interaction with some descendants of John D Rockefeller when I was in Hobart in 2003, buying an investment property to be developed.

At the time I was invited to an art show in Hobart, which turned out to be the city's social event of the year. When I entered the gallery, I even felt a little under-dressed. This was a who's who gathering of Hobart society.

After an hour or two of mingling in the crowd, I noticed two elderly gentlemen sitting in comfortable chairs in a corner, enjoying some very large tumblers of whisky. They looked interesting so I went to join them. It turned out they were Rockefeller descendants living quietly in Hobart, having changed their names to avoid the spotlight. They had bought large slabs of land in Hobart when it was dirt cheap, long before that property market took off.

They had moved to Hobart for lifestyle, but once they got there, they saw the chance to leverage a number of property investment opportunities. Compared to Manhattan, Hobart was a fraction of the price and still offered water views. They had even bought some properties in Salamanca Place, home of the famous Salamanca Market.

Interestingly, over a whisky or two, we got to talking about the connection Hobart has to the man many consider Australia's greatest entrepreneur, Kerry Francis Bullmore Packer.

Packer mentioned a few times in interviews before his death, that his grandfather, Robert Clyde Packer, went to the races in Hobart and found 10 pounds on the ground. He put the money on a 10–1 long shot and the horse galloped home. Using his winnings, Robert bought a ticket to Sydney and went into the newspaper industry—and did quite well. That is how the Packer empire started: with 10 bob on a racehorse!

While we cannot all win at the horse races (and most lose), this is a pertinent example of someone not only fully leveraging their capital, but also not spending all their bonus gains on some immediate personal indulgence and instead looking for an opportunity to invest those funds.

In the Packer family's case, it was the bourgeoning newspaper industry of the 1950s.

Today, it could be building an app that allows you to test for health conditions using your mobile phone.

In the end, taking control is something that is critical, whether it be in our investment strategies or in how we manage our time.

Amazon founder Jeff Bezos has one key takeaway for his success. He says it's having an 'obsessive compulsive focus on the customer'. Of course, you might say 'everyone in business says that'. What does that mean in its essence? It means having empathy for the people you are trying to sell something to using whatever channel you choose. It means deeply understanding what you are trying to achieve and that requires hard work, research and focus. All these are themes that we will keep coming back to in this book.

I would also like to remind you that Amazon shares went public at \$US18 each on 15 May 1997, a value that initially fell after several stock splits in the years that followed in 1998 and 1999.

Various analysts have calculated what \$US1000 in those shares would be worth today if you had bought during the IPO and still held them. Depending on share price changes, those shares in Australian dollar terms would be worth close to \$2 million. Not bad for a loss-making online book seller back in 1997.

2. Investment leverage

We can all put money aside each month and save towards an investment fund, which is a good idea, but that can take considerable time. Leveraging for investment purposes—known as 'buying on margin'—can be a powerful tool for exponentially increasing returns, although using leverage to invest can also be risky. Worst-case scenario is that losses can increase, and when the value of the securities doesn't match the loan, money will have to be found elsewhere to meet your obligations to the lender.

What happens when investors choose this pathway is they create a margin account with an agreed lender, and then use that account to buy and sell company stock or shares, or sometimes other forms of security. Margin accounts are one of the main types of investment leverage.

The advantage of this type of leverage is that you can buy more shares or other types of securities than if you were using your own money—so the returns are potentially significantly greater. For the borrower, the value of the shares or securities offers the collateral for the loan, so if they decline significantly, the lender might call in the loan and force you to sell the shares. In addition, the broker will charge interest.

Why do investors do it? Well, typically a broker will allow an investor to borrow up to 50–70 per cent of the face of the share or security (those shares they approve, anyway) meaning together with your own money you can double your purchasing power in the amount of stock you can purchase. In effect you're getting double the bang for your buck — assuming the securities appreciate in value over time.

The flip side is if the value of the securities falls. What happens then is your broker might make a margin call? What does this mean? Investors will typically be required to pay more money into the account to meet minimum equity obligations. Sometimes, the broker might sell some of your shares without your permission to achieve that outcome as well.

Other ways to use debt to invest

While margin lending is the most common way to buy and sell stocks or other forms of securities, it isn't the only way. Some people, usually the more sophisticated investors, take out loans or other lines of credit to invest in the market as well.

The strategy here is to build up a lump sum to generate a greater return or to create a more diversified portfolio, which in general terms is a good thing to aim to achieve.

Sometimes, it doesn't amount to huge borrowing: some brokers allow investors to purchase fractional shares of funds, with a starting point as low as $500, which of course can always be topped up at a later stage.

Other debt-based investing strategies include:

- *Taking out a personal loan*

  Sometimes people would prefer to use an unsecured personal loan to buy and sell securities. This has the advantage that you don't require property as collateral (so you don't jeopardise the value of your house), but it can involve higher interest rates than mortgage rates (so your investment fund will need higher returns to cover the higher interest). Additionally, lenders are much tougher about who they will lend unsecured personal loans to for investment. It helps, of course, if you have a very good credit rating or a relationship with the lender, such as a good record of meeting your mortgage repayments.

  If you're careful with how you manage your cash flow, this is another alternative for generating the funds to build an investment portfolio.

- *Using the equity in your home*

  The equity in your home can be used as a line of credit. We all know that your home is your greatest financial asset, and should never be risked, but it is also often a very valuable asset that isn't generating you a day-to-day return, apart from hopefully appreciating in value day after day. Some people use the equity in their home to either take out a home equity line of credit (HELOC), which attracts its own interest rate, or just a straight home equity loan (which might attract a straight mortgage rate of interest) to create an investment pool. Let's be clear: this is on the riskier side of the leverage equation because the consequences for your home can be significant if the value of the investment portfolio declines, but if you can keep up with the repayments it is something to consider.

- *Using your credit card cash advance*

  Typically, credit cards attract high interest rates for those who don't pay off their monthly balances, but if you have a low-interest credit card, another option is to create a cash advance for investment purposes. Just remember there are other pitfalls along the way as the credit card provider will probably require a higher annual percentage rate (APR) than for typical credit card purchases and may charge cash advance fees, too. A high APR, or interest paid on the cash advance, means there is more pressure for your investment portfolio to achieve higher returns to meet your financial commitments.

3. Personal finance leverage

We all leverage when it comes to enhancing our personal finances. Everything from pulling our credit card out when we've had dinner to thinking about how we're going to finance our next car.

Essentially, each time you borrow money to buy an asset you're leveraging. If you take out a mortgage to buy a house, you're leveraging. Even taking out a student loan to educate yourself with the end result of landing a well-paid job is leveraging. Acquiring an asset such as a car is important for how we manage our work and daily lives, so it significantly adds to our productivity. However, cars generally lose value over time, though they are often essential for getting us to and from work to earn an income.

Just remember that going into debt to leverage isn't something you should do lightly. You should always anticipate interest rate changes in forecasting your cash flow, and there are serious consequences if you can't meet your repayments. Not only do you lose the asset you've purchased, but it will have a significant impact on your credit status. This means the next time you want to borrow money for something critical you might be declined. While financial leveraging is a way to dramatically improve your financial standing, make sure you think before you leap.

4. Professional trading leverage

The primary occupation of professional investors and traders is to trade securities. As such, they generally conduct extensive research and devote more time to understanding investment trends. Consequently, they are more inclined to take on higher levels of leverage when investing in stocks or other forms of security.

Professional traders, especially those with a good track record or affiliated with their own investment fund, are not subject to the same constraints as average mum-and-dad investors. For example, a Forex broker employed by one of the big banks could request orders 500 times the size of their initial deposit.

These traders are happy to leverage because they can get in and out of stock positions strategically to (hopefully) to seize new opportunities and mitigate potential declines in their portfolios. Debt, in their case, offers the means to significantly amplify their purchasing power for investment purposes, which is a deliberate choice stemming from their commitment to the profession of trading.

It is important to acknowledge that a greater disparity between available cash and margin means a more substantial potential of greater returns and losses, especially when linked to large orders.

This is a markedly distinct world for most investors and best navigated by experienced traders.

Leverage danger zone

Humans have been using financial leverage for as long as there has been trade. Before there were currencies, people bartered. When coins began circulating, well before Christ—particularly gold and silver coins—some individuals were able to hoard them and lend them to others. Today, borrowing is far more sophisticated and the availability of cash plenty, but there are still dangers.

While financial leverage is the only way most people can afford to buy a home, with commitments also come obligations, starting with keeping up the interest payments and then paying off the principal loan.

Leveraging for investment can be particularly lucrative if you pick the right asset to purchase and it increases in value—at least by more than the value you borrowed. Property investment has traditionally been successful in mature economies such as Australia because it has been a relatively stable asset class.

Stock markets have also generally increased in value over time—although of course individual stocks may dramatically vary in value, and over decades many former blue-chip stocks have completely disappeared.

There is one other big danger where inexperienced investors in particular can fall into a trap. This is by not following the leader, but 'following the follower'. What does this mean?

A prime example is cryptocurrency. When a company or an asset class such as Bitcoin receives significant media hype or is heavily marketed, investors are tempted to follow without giving factors such as the tax implications much thought.

According to the Australian Taxation Office (ATO), as at 30 June 2023 there were 612 549 crypto trading accounts in Australia, most of which were actively trading. (There may have been others that the ATO wasn't aware of.) An estimated 98 per cent of traders globally have no idea how digital currency works, nor what buying or selling actually involves. Even worse, they were likely not aware that any big wins would be detected by the ATO.

Data matching is easier to monitor than most people think. Ironically, most of these novice traders won't need to worry about the ATO issuing them with a notice that the digital trades weren't declared on their tax returns. Why? Most of the traders today are sitting with capital losses anyway. Dumb!

As most investors aren't clued up to understand and measure risk for themselves, they leave it to an advisor, an institution or even worse the government, by leaving their funds in super or a retirement plan.

What are the costs and penalties of leaving it to someone else to do?

In short, you're paying significant fees to others. Studies have shown that fees in financial broking, funds management, individual retirement accounts (IRAs), superannuation and listed managed funds can see between 18 and 20 per cent stripped from your earnings. This has been the cost to investors and today most members are oblivious to what is still occurring. Sadly, 99 per cent of the Western world are asleep at the wheel.

Let's put it in some context. If you rent out a property today your real estate agent might say their charge to manage the property is about 6 per cent of the rental cost. Now imagine if they said that cost is going up to 18 per cent. What would your response or action be on the back of receiving that news?

That's what has transpired for 60 years in the United States, Europe and Australia, where fund managers have been deducting ridiculously high fees from investors' funds. What is even more concerning is that the recent bout of higher global inflation is also eating into your savings. This means you could be losing at both ends of the financial equation.

Collectively, the point is that your capital is being gouged, and when coupled with higher-than-average inflation (which is stripping the spending power of your investments), in many cases this means you will never ever have enough to retire on. See figures 1.1 and 1.2.

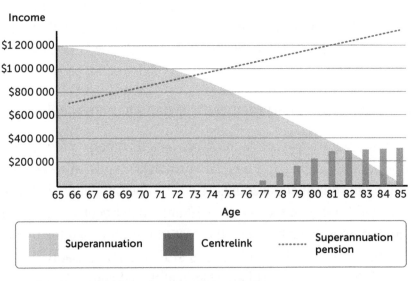

Figure 1.1: financial reserves over time—males

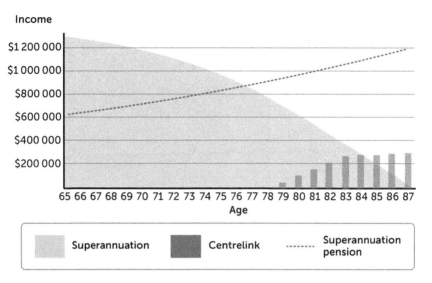

Figure 1.2: financial reserves over time—females

For those who think the aged pension is there to save you, think again. Governments—more so today, in the post-pandemic era—are in a precarious financial position due to too much money having been printed in recent years and are not thinking through or initiating a long-term management plan. They have directed too much of the country's taxpayer money in the wrong areas of need. That means budgets are dealing with major debt repayments.

Throw in stagnant wage growth in the Western world and the impact on spending power, and it might not be as powerful today as it was 50 years ago. On top of that are the impacts on mental health and wellbeing and it's no wonder that people feel pessimistic about the future.

According to the US Bureau of Labor Statistics, between 1970 and 2023 the buying power of $1 reduced dramatically. Figures 1.3 and 1.4 (overleaf) demonstrate the real challenge: we need more and more invested capital to retire comfortably, and our spending power is diminishing through higher inflation.

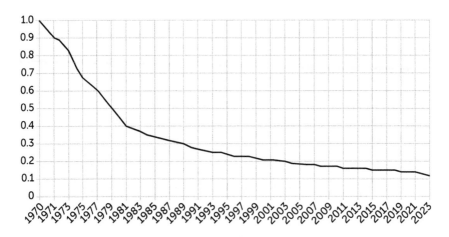

Figure 1.3: the buying power of $1 over time, 1970–2023

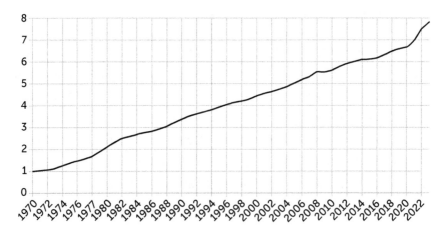

Figure 1.4: $1 in 1970, adjusted for inflation

Figure 1.5 shows the average annual rate of inflation for select CPI categories.

As the cost of living rises, compared to a stagnant income, coupled with a less attractive retirement savings system, more people are feeling they are falling behind and failing financially.

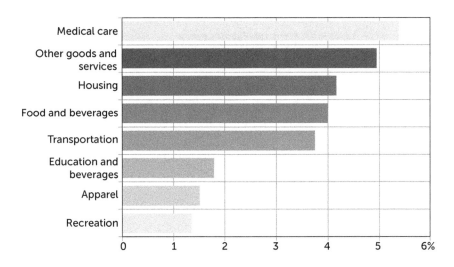

Figure 1.5: inflation by category (%)

It's time to take control and not just follow the boom-and-bust cycle of jumping on the latest hot stocks and then trying to jump out again.

LET'S REFLECT ...

- Financial leverage—borrowing money to invest—can be a powerful tool for supercharging your investment or business growth.

- Intelligent leveraging is about doing your research, engaging with others and properly managing your time and resources.

- While the tax advantages of leveraging should be factored in, tax outcomes should not be the foundation of your investment strategy.

- Seek professional help so that you're aware of shifts in financial markets, changes in government policies and interest rate changes.

- There are costs associated with borrowing, especially in a rising interest rate environment, so proceed carefully and do not 'follow the follower' into investments that are recommended by the media without doing the right research.

- Take control. Leaving it to your financial adviser or the government comes with costs as well as higher fees. Think about how much money you'll really need to retire.

CHAPTER <u>2</u>

SUPERANNUATION: TOO SLOW, TOO RISKY, TOO EXPENSIVE

Here is a wake-up call: don't go through life thinking retirement will look after itself. When it comes to retirement savings, Australia is fortunate to have a compulsory superannuation system. It does force everyone to put savings aside for when they are no longer working. But it is not the Holy Grail that many people believe it is and cannot be relied upon on its own to secure your financial future. The sad reality is that most people now think super alone will look after them in retirement and they switch off.

A range of factors is eating into the lucrative superannuation pie: costs, taxes, and advisor or accountancy fees all impact the return on your investment.

I often look at the superannuation sector, with its $3.6 trillion plus undermanagement, as the fat seal that all the sharks try to feed off.

And it's likely to get worse—governments and institutions will slowly, unwittingly and subtly chip away at your retirement savings.

What the COVID-19 pandemic has done in many respects is brought forward 10 years of the inevitable regarding the structural challenges facing macro-economics and sectors such as superannuation when it comes to industry rationalisation and change.

In 2023, Australia's retirement savings amounted to about $3.6 trillion, but now in the post-pandemic world Australia's national debt stands at about one-third of this figure. Prior to the Global Financial Crisis (GFC) in 2007, according to Australian Government data, the Australian Government's gross debt was $52 billion and in 2023 it was at $923 billion.

Due to low productivity government initiatives, particularly in Australia, coupled with the sale of many great tax-income-generating assets to China and the rest of the world, governments are likely to be forced to borrow more money in the future and the cost of servicing this debt will impact income taxes, probably followed by adjusting the tax concessions on superannuation, which has already started happening for higher income earners with balances of more than $3 million.

Other taxes are under review as well, such as the capital gains concessions on assets, as part of a huge overhaul by the Australian Government. This will see a switch from super to trusts. Super needs a continuing flow of funds to meet future obligations, especially as the baby boomers retire in the next decade.

On top of that is the pressure on governments—both state and federal—to access the billions of dollars of funds in superannuation (especially industry-based super controlled by unions) and to channel those funds into infrastructure building or social housing spending to take some pressure off the budget.

A recent article in the *Australian Financial Review (AFR)* all but laid out the plans by the federal government, which are likely to receive largely bipartisan support because most governments of all persuasions are broke.

The 2022 *AFR* article outlines how Australian Treasurer Dr Jim Chalmers told a business round table that super played a role in investing in Australia's priorities and 'addressing some of our most formidable economic challenges'.

'We see trillions of dollars in workers' capital, we see government budgets heaving with debt, and there are obvious needs for investment, particularly in areas like housing and energy'. Dr Chalmers told the annual superannuation lending roundtable hosted by the AFR and packaging multinational Visy, that 'reform' and 'new ideas' are being welcomed.

Find the best returns

Sucking funds out of super for projects under government direction means less liquidity for super funds to invest them into assets that could produce higher returns elsewhere. Some of these projects would also attract high debt, which would be linked to your savings. Then there is the question of whether the asset makes an adequate return. This is the increased risk with this strategy. History tells us that governments both here in Australia and in the United States have proven to be very, very poor at allocation and return on capital.

If you just follow the follower again—this time by hoping the super sector looks after itself—then you are losing control. Instead, let's get an investment you can control, and where you know what the tax implications are for you.

For the Federal Government itself, the super system is also becoming unsustainable. A 2023 Grattan Institute report revealed that the superannuation sector costs $45 billion a year in foregone government revenue and will soon exceed the cost of the age pension: 'These tax breaks are excessively generous—extending well beyond any plausible purpose for our superannuation system to provide for income in retirement—and their costs are unsustainable'.

Behind the scenes, the entire Australian retirement savings of $3.6 trillion is slowly but forcefully being compressed from over 12 000 managed funds now registered according to the Australian Securities & Investments Commission (ASIC) in Australia and 145 APRA-regulated super funds to just a dozen or more (mostly) industry funds. There are 23.2 million open super accounts—this is a frightening thought in its own right given that this number almost equals Australia's population. Ultimately, this is taking control away from the members. Super is slowly evolving into the biggest government and institutional con of the past 75 years.

In 2023, Treasurer Chalmers admitted to the *AFR* that the superannuation sector was at an 'inflection point' and said the sector had to 'work harder to deliver steady income for the millions of baby boomers entering retirement and to explain why annuities have not been taken up with sufficient enthusiasm'.

In the same report, the *AFR* wrote that former Labor prime minister Paul Keating, the architect of Australia's super system, acknowledged that the equities-focused compulsory super system needed to turn to investments that 'deliver a fixed income to meet demographic and inflation challenges'.

If the next likely move means governments encouraging or incentivising superannuation members to lend their funds to help finance government-related projects, the result will mean more government control of our savings pool.

My experience in helping manage funds for others has been that using trusts and/or special purchase vehicles for asset protection and wealth building has allowed access to the endless assets available globally and has the leveraging power to use debt via your bank.

Let's compare the options of using super to other forms of investment.

For example, if you had $500 000 today in superannuation and were hoping the fund you've selected could achieve the past 15 years' average of 9 per cent compounding return, then that equates to a balance of $1 183 681 in 10 years' time. If you assume the employer or an average additional annual contribution to your fund is $15 000 per year, that total comes to $1 411 575 in a decade (see figure 2.1). That sounds okay, doesn't it?

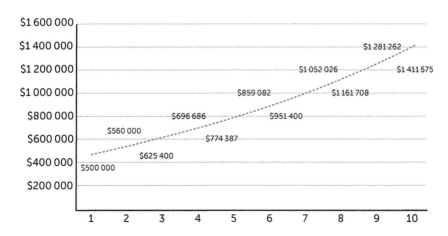

Figure 2.1: chart of gearing

Now, consider the alternative. What if you were to gear those funds either with real estate, global shares or any well-proven asset class over the same period, using the same $500 000 capital pool. Assume you can use your own salary of, say, $15 000 to service interest costs (assuming a rate of 6 per cent per annum, which is tax deductible — for now at least) and using a net rental income of $36 000 on an investment property, that would enable you to borrow $650 000 on top of your $500 000 capital base. Over 10 years, the same metrics on return on investment and assumed risks creates a nest egg outcome of $2 722 468.

Now that's a 'compare the pair', as the superannuation industry likes to say.

Even if the property achieves an annual return of 5 per cent, the end value after 10 years is still $1 873 228.

In short, in Australia as well as other Western nations, superannuation or other forms of retirement savings systems are becoming far too restrictive and too controlled, preventing access to the growth and endless global assets available today.

After managing billions for clients over the years, I believe there is still too much fat in the institutions and what is stripped by the investors' instalments. In summary, superannuation is too slow, too expensive, too restrictive and too risky.

Avoid the super trap

Plan, plan, plan, and never stop planning to take control. You had better think about the future because that's where you will be living!

Let's be clear, superannuation is important, but the mismanagement by government and the financial institutions that regulate superannuation have mostly positioned themselves to control our savings into a platform that is not always in the best interests of the tax-paying citizens and it's something that cannot be accessed.

Sadly, superannuation has become an advice and distribution circus trap. At its worst, the retirement savings architecture has become a big casino for governments and institutions, without the lights and cabaret show.

The advice and the reporting industry that circles this multibillion-dollar market today doesn't call out the alternatives, which means investors are mostly ignorant and don't understand the game of finance and investment instruments.

Many of the best investments I have ever made were, and still are, not even listed or investment regulated. For example, investment property, which has incidentally performed fabulously over the past 50 years, particularly here in Australia.

But good luck trying to get an advisor to recommend investment property as part of a portfolio. Why? Because they can't report or wrap their management services around that asset, as the investor has too much influence and control over the asset—and that's why institutions and regulators can't make a dollar from unlisted real estate despite it being one of the best asset classes in the history of the Western world. Their response is often, 'It's not on our approved list!'

There is life after managed funds or the stock exchange. Of course, let's be clear that real wealth takes decades of hard work, but the key takeaway for all investors is simple: *make it, keep it and leverage it!*

Do your research

It's not easy, but investing into careful and time-consuming research is worth it. There is nothing like doing it yourself, but there are some options for seeking out non-aligned independent experts in investment who will charge a one-off fee to provide the best-known returns over the past 20 to 50 years of all instruments with supporting data. Now that's a great investment of funds.

Keeping up to date means spending a few hours less each week on social media or watching TV and seeking out credible material that might catapult you closer to your financial destiny and goals 10 to 15 years earlier.

One thing to always look out for when managing your own investments is what's called 'counterparty' risks. A counterparty risk is where a party to a transaction either defaults or doesn't deliver on its expected rate of return.

To mitigate against counterparty risks I engage advisers and experts—whether it be the director or, in the case of superannuation, investment teams—to oversee performance. That all costs money. I call them touch points and each one charges a fee. My estimate is that these have cost investors, in most cases, an average of 18 to 20 per cent of their returns over the course of the investment period.

But it's not just super. This also applies to yield returns and expenses inside a range of investments: fixed interest, term deposits, international fixed interest, listed property trusts, unlisted property trusts, Australian share portfolios and international shares. The areas that can impact returns include buy–sell spread, interest, cost ratios, management expense ratios, trustee fees, custodial fees and management fees — and they have been excessive for far too long. The expenses related to these investments could cost a serious investor as much as one million dollars over the course of 20 years. That all has a major impact on your retirement income plans.

Watch out for mutual funds and any managed investment coupled to industry funds, which seems to be commonplace now. This is the easiest space to park money for masses of people or investors who don't have to or, more importantly, don't want to, manage it themselves.

It is important to note these investments require the least amount of thought and can be established by a 15 year old without even so much as a drivers licence, but might equally appeal to a doctor or lawyer in their 40s. These investments are pre-packed and designed for precisely the purpose of giving you no discretion on the underlying investments. It's like ordering a meal at McDonald's: there is a pre-set menu, and the consumer gets little say in the outcome.

These managed funds and any managed investment in particular institutions have done a wonderful marketing job on the masses. Index funds targeting assets such as gold, silver, real estate and direct shares have done so well, yet have the lowest level of fees associated with that direct investment due to less handling and touch points on such investments. Just watch out for hidden costs.

LET'S REFLECT ...

- Superannuation is a great tool for forced savings and to ensure you have a retirement plan, but it is becoming too controlled and the returns are less predictable.

- Costs, taxes, and advisor or accountancy fees all impact the return on your super investment.

- A tax overhaul by the Australian Government is likely to result in a switch from super to trusts.

- Watch for fees and other 'third party risks' or hidden fees when considering your retirement plan.

- Plan—and never stop planning—to take control and consider investment alternatives using leveraging to boost your total returns.

- The key point for any investor is simple: make it, keep it and leverage it!

CHAPTER <u>3</u>

LAND AND RESIDENTIAL PROPERTY: YOUR BEST INVESTMENT

I have known a wise businessman for over 30 years, and we were recently discussing how he became so wealthy. It seemed effortless for him, while he openly displayed being the happiest and most joyful person I've ever come across. At the time, he controlled three gold mines and large land holdings throughout Europe and the United States, and had a particular interest in diamond trading. He told me he believed that people are generally lost today. He explained that people didn't have the vaguest idea about what they really want while on this 'holiday on earth'.

People tend to just fall into their vocation without much prior thought. He went on to tell me that his wealth was largely built on demand for goods and how he could make a difference to help others. Most importantly, his wealth first started from the ground, from the dirt or, more accurately, what lay beneath it.

He was referring to the general principle that everyone's prime requirement stems from the need for food and shelter—and both come from the ground.

His comments have had a profound impact on my own thinking. I now look down to the ground when making decisions before I look up. I agree that's where the foundation of all things begin.

My friend talked of earlier days, his experiences during World War II and their impact on him as well as his family and friends. The legacy was an emotional and physical desire to obtain permanent and galvanised security and wellbeing. His desire was driven by never ever being in such a vulnerable position again as he was in World War II, faced with the threat to Jewish people in Europe.

It's not surprising, then, that research indicates that Jewish investors hold a significant portion of the world's gold and silver holdings today.

The blatantly obvious need for the essentials of land, food and shelter and a desire to acquire the building blocks of economic development such as coal, oil and gas have been with us for generations. Gold and silver, without the dependence on the rapidly devaluating dollars printed on paper as currency, has always been a form of bartering.

Owning something physical also removes any interference of counterparty costs and manipulation. These assets can be directly controlled without the risk of being placed or forced into the hands of another counterparty.

This all goes back to the fundamentals of investment: owning something that is in limited supply and is likely to rise in value if demand is maintained, particularly if it's important for human survival.

The growing 'rental generation'

This brings me back to land and property. In Australia, the family home has for the past 30 years been any household's best investment. It's non tax deductible and helps build wealth given the general capital growth seen over decades. The bottom line is no-one can produce more land, apart from limited attempts to reclaim land from the sea, for the creation of physical property, because there is not an endless supply.

But property acquisition statistics, especially in relation to home ownership, are rapidly changing and investors will need to adapt to those changes as well.

According to a 2022 Australian Housing and Urban Research Institute (AHURI) report, home ownership rates have seemingly remained almost static over the past 30 years, despite the challenges of Australia's altered institutional environment, including market moves (increased prices making it harder to enter the market) and demographic shifts. The Australian Bureau of Statistics (ABS) census results show that home ownership was at 67 per cent in 2016, compared to 68 per cent in 1976 and 66 per cent in 2021. This steadiness in ownership levels is mainly due to the baby boomer generation, who were eager to secure a home as early as possible after World War II.

However, the AHURI reports that Australia is unlikely to be able to sustain these home ownership levels, saying that home ownership is projected to decline to around 63 per cent overall by 2040, and, of particular significance, to just over 50 per cent — down from 60 per cent in 1981 — for those aged 25 to 55.

This decline will most likely be driven by factors such as the overprovision of apartments (more suited to renters than owners), stagnation of the Australian labour market and affordability.

This trend was also noted in research results published in 2022 by Global Property Research (GPR), which found that home ownership is falling in many developed countries, mainly 'market liberal' countries such as Australia. The exceptions were Germany, France and the Netherlands.

For Australia this means shifting to an increasingly dual tenure society: ownership and (private and social) rental.

Prospective home owners will be compelled to rethink their home ownership strategy, and governments and policymakers will have no option but to reconsider existing housing and related policies.

All of this has socio-economic ramifications for future generations and increases the risk of a disparity between owners and renters. It isn't all doom and gloom though, as renters without a mortgage (assuming they have spare discretionary income) can pursue opportunities to create wealth in other ways, especially if they are encouraged by government policy such as super.

There will also be a likely process of ageing homeowners redistributing some of their asset-generated wealth to the next generation to help them get into the property market.

If the 'Australian dream' of owning your own home becomes unattainable, this will have significant implications for future investors wanting to accumulate land and property because, make no mistake, this asset class will remain attractive as a capital generating asset given the predictions of population growth across Australia, mainly driven by immigration. The bottom line is we all need somewhere to live.

The impact will be felt mostly by those in the 24 to 45 age group, whose ability to purchase property has decreased, mainly due to affordability as well as income stagnation, particularly among the lower income quintiles of this cohort.

This trend is exacerbated by an increase in remote work and the gig economy, which is influencing where people choose to live and their ability to purchase a home.

Shifts in property investment strategies

The property market is responding to the rise of the 'rental generation' as well with a boom in so-called 'build-to-rent' multi-unit dwellings, especially in Australia's major capital cities, which will restrict stock for traditional owner-occupiers.

The build-to-rent era, a phrase no-one had even heard of just a few years ago (even though it has been popular in the United States for many years) is here to stay in Australia. This hybrid model, whereby tenants can eventually buy into their build-to-rent apartment, once they are in a financial position to do so, is likely to become more popular in the future

What does this mean for those still wanting to get into the property sector? For some it means buying an apartment, if they can afford it, rather than a house. For others, who may be working in or near the Central Business District (CBD), it means looking to regional Australia to buy an investment property—where there is a healthy rental market as tenants tend to take advantage of lower rates—and renting near where they work.

With a smaller outlay on a regional property these buyers can more quickly pay off their mortgage with their rental income and more quickly own an asset that they could sell to allow them to buy something closer to a major capital. The alternative of having a very large mortgage and trying to live near one of the main cities means it will take so much longer to pay off their debts and they might struggle if interest rates remain higher than average.

There are several types of investment options that now lie ahead for people wanting to own a form of shelter—it's certainly less straight forward than it used to be to gain a foothold in the property sector and build wealth, but it is still achievable. One way is not to move into your first property, but to stay at home with Mum and Dad and let the rent pay off the mortgage for as long as possible to bring it down, or consider inter-generational living. That's where parents and children choose to share the costs of home ownership and jointly share the title.

Remember all the costs that are associated with residential investment—including ongoing body corporate fees if it is an apartment or unit—and maintenance costs on the property are largely tax deductible.

Others might never consider buying property at all, but would rather rent and put any spare income they have towards other forms of investment, which if accumulated, could one day be put towards property.

To come back to our key theme of intelligent leverage, property investors of tomorrow are going to have to do far more research, work more closely with their lenders to look for options and even think about opportunities to leverage intergenerational wealth.

We are at a tipping point for housing investment in Australia, and the market will need to respond to changing consumer and investor requirements.

For investors, there will always be demand for private rental, especially given the projections for population growth in Australia's major capital cities. If the stock of the private rental market doesn't improve, yields will remain high for investors. So far it is mainly institutional investors, seeking the long-term rental returns, who are moving into the 'build-to-rent' sector. It's also possible that there will be more intergenerational investment in housing, as well as parents or grandparents helping out first homebuyers to get into the market.

Clearly, changes to the way we live to allow greater density in inner-city areas where there is already infrastructure will require shifts in planning and new forms of private–public investment.

No doubt this will also require governments to modify existing policies around home ownership grants, tax reform, housing assistance and possibly deregulating planning systems to fast-track approvals to improve the housing stock and drive down prices.

Not every sector will be the same, nor will it be identical for every city or even suburb in Australia. What that means again is *plan, research and use your leverage* wherever you can.

There will also likely be a major shift and policy changes to industrial and commercial land as retail fundamentally changes over the next 20 years.

Repurposing commercial property

Remember, it isn't just residential property where investors have flocked over generations. Commercial property has been the mainstay of many balanced asset portfolios for investors, but this too is about to undergo its own revolution, driven by changing retail patterns.

The commercial real estate market looks like it will be forever changed as the COVID-19 pandemic leaves lasting impacts. It's impacted the way traditional office buildings will be utilised by employees, it's changed retail forever and sped up the uptake in online shopping—which impacts everything from shopping centres to strip shopping—and it's changed the way people interact with the CBD.

The commercial property market and the landlords and investors who own these properties will have to become smarter to deal with the escalating work-from-home (WFH) trend, increase in e-commerce and huge population movement within Australia.

Maintaining building occupancy is a growing concern for owners of commercial real estate as rents decline. We only have to look at Melbourne and Sydney in particular to see vacant commercial properties. Vacant properties pose additional risks for owners because it isn't just the loss of income, but maintenance and fire risks also increase in empty buildings.

This will inevitably mean many buildings will need to be repurposed into apartment living or those still likely to attract workers will need fresh amenities to satisfy new workplace norms and encourage hybrid working spaces.

As such, business owners and investors need to find ways of keeping their buildings functioning.

Investors, including those investing in property funds, are going to have to be nimble in effectively navigating these changes, leveraging every opportunity they can to prosper.

And the clock is ticking for many investors. As buildings become ever more vacant, property fund returns will decline and the costs to maintain those buildings will rise, especially if they face vandalism or theft. That, of course, only compounds the cost of commercial property insurance and when you're not taking in rental income, there are fewer opportunities to take advantage of expense tax opportunities.

As the *Nationwide* website contends: 'Therefore, it's crucial for businesses [or private investors] that own commercial properties to take steps to keep their buildings occupied and avoid vacancy issues'.

It's clear, especially with the current housing shortage, that the popular method for commercial property owners to repurpose their building will be to target residential apartment living.

For this option the building shell is already in place, which should reduce the building costs, depending on the internal configuration. It is also possible to have multiple tenant uses in a repurposed building, such as having a café or small retail space on the ground floor, apartments on some of the floors above and a possible rooftop bar or restaurant on the top floor.

The biggest determinant of costs would be the installation of balconies (which in the post-COVID era most people refer to as 'access to fresh air') and the plumbing fit-out of additional bathrooms and kitchens for apartment living.

In fact, it is clear that not all commercial properties can be repurposed to residential living. There are limitations due to the original design of the building or heritage as well as other factors that would make it more difficult.

The open-plan structure of shopping malls and some office buildings would significantly add to the costs of creating sub-divided living. Commercial property owners and property funds will need to analyse their facilities carefully before making any remodelling decisions.

There will be many hurdles to clear before our cities transform from office hubs to living spaces. These include:

- Every council in Australia has different planning and building codes that will need to be followed. The building codes when it comes to fire protection, smoke detectors, exit and entry points, evacuation points, disability access and types of materials to be used in residential apartments are often more stringent than in office buildings. Ensuring that a repurposed building adheres to all these regulations can add to the costs of refitting a building.

- Utilities such as water, electrics, lighting and especially plumbing are likely to need upgrades or improvements. Usually, an office building will only have one set of toilets (male, female and ambulant) per floor, but if it's converted into five or six apartments, that might mean 10 or more toilets, six kitchens, six bathrooms and other water outlets. The daily water use of an apartment building is significantly higher than that of an office building.

- There is the issue of whether to retrograde fit balconies to office buildings that don't usually have them so that apartment occupiers can slide open their doors and step outside. This has become something of a must-have for most apartment owners and increases the size and value of apartments when selling or renting.

- Sprinkler systems and other fire protection features would need to be upgraded. When a commercial office space is built, the number of sprinklers installed is dependent on the number of inhabitants and layout of the building. This would significantly change in an apartment building.

- The types of materials used in constructing commercial buildings might have been approved at the time of construction but may now not be considered safe and may possibly be combustible.

- Typically, office buildings might not have the car parking spaces required for apartment living, nor would they likely have the storage facilities (such as storage cages) required by apartment dwellers. These would both need to be added to any construction plans and would both reduce the space for a commercial return from building new apartments.

- There will no doubt be different ongoing insurance, maintenance and concierge costs associated with having an apartment building, compared with an office building. Depending on the sale process, some of these costs would be offset by owner's corporation fees, but the building owner would still likely be liable for some of these costs.

And it isn't only the likelihood of commercial buildings being repurposed for residential use that will have a major impact on investors. Business owners who moved to e-commerce due to the COVID-19 restrictions may well like to convert their shop to a warehouse or distribution centre where they can store their goods.

Major industrial property has also become hot thanks to the e-commerce boom as local and global operators such as Amazon build new fulfilment centres. Investors will be closely following this trend to see if their property funds are major investors in these mega new centres.

The COVID-19 pandemic undeniably played a significant role in bringing about extensive transformations and exposing vulnerabilities within the commercial property sector. By recognising these challenges and proactively addressing them, businesses can thrive in the midst of this dynamic and evolving landscape.

LET'S REFLECT ...

- Residential property has been the best investment for most households over many generations, but the sector is becoming harder to access and requires new entrants or investors to do more research and consider their options.

- The fundamentals of investment involve owning something that is in limited supply and is likely to rise in value if demand is maintained, particularly if it's important for human survival.

- Property acquisition statistics in relation to home ownership are rapidly declining and investors need to adapt to these changes.

- The rise of the 'rental generation' and a boom in 'build-to-rent' multi-unit dwellings will restrict stock for traditional owner-occupiers.

- Future investors will have to do more research, work more closely with their lenders to look for options and possibly think about opportunities to leverage intergenerational wealth.

- Leverage the opportunities you have with family support, thinking about buying property in the regions, or embrace renting and put aside spare income into other forms of investment.

- Changes to the way we live to allow greater density in inner-city areas where there is already infrastructure will require shifts in planning and new forms of private–public investment.

- Commercial and industrial property will go through its own transformation for investors, and will need to be carefully navigated.

- Plan, research and use your leverage wherever you can.

CHAPTER 4

SHARES: THEIR IMPORTANCE IN THE INVESTMENT MIX

Owning stocks is a way for investors to grab their share of a corporate growth story. The benefits are clear. If there are capital gains and franked dividends paid, investors can not only protect their money from inflation and taxes, but they can maximise their income. Returns in shares can easily outperform other forms of investment, but let's also be clear, shares can be among the riskiest form of investment any investor can make.

Drawing on the data I have collected on the past 75 years of share investments in the United States and Australia, the returns overall have been strong.

Shares in these two markets have offered a return on investment of 21 655.68 per cent over that period, or 10.58 per cent per year. Research by Hamilton-Chase Pty Ltd in 2023 found that this lump-sum investment beats inflation during the same period for an inflation-adjusted return of about 2661.35 per cent cumulatively, or 6.40 per cent per year.

These are the best performing companies in stock-market history, according to Admirals Markets:

- Coca-Cola (NASDAQ: KO)

- Altria (NASDAQ: MO)

- Amazon.com (NASDAQ: AMZN)

- Celgene (NASDAQ: CELG)

- Apple (NASDAQ: AAPL)

- Alphabet (NASDAQ: GOOG)

- Gilead Sciences (NASDAQ: GILD)

- Microsoft (NASDAQ: MSFT).

Consider this: if you nailed investing in even half of the companies mentioned above (and avoided the other 250 stocks in a normal traditional balanced fund) that would result in a return of 42.34 per cent per annum more than the mix of the 250 stocks in a bundled portfolio mutual fund.

Of course we cannot always pick winners. In a fund of 250 stocks, probably half of them would not be around over the next 20 years. Having said that, it is always better to take the hard long-term game—with a 10-, 20- or even 35-year horizon.

As I've already mentioned, over the past 75 years in excess of 87 per cent of the companies in the S&P US index have been taken over, gone broke and/or been delisted.

The good news is that looking at the next three to five years, I believe shares in Australia, Japan and the United States look very cheap—certainly compared to real estate, which will be further impacted by the elevated federal and state government tax and other charges associated with the post-pandemic budget recovery plans. The flow of capital away from property to shares will inevitably help share prices.

While higher bond yields are weighing on stocks, there will be opportunities in shares in the coming years. Blue chip stocks will see earnings grow as economic growth recovers (as interest rates globally start to decline again), especially for those companies without high overheads, or that have already been through the digital transformation, or don't face high capital costs to remain competitive.

Top 10 accounting metrics for share investing

The key to intelligent stock-market investing is to understand some of the key accounting KPIs (Key Performance Indicators) that drive a company's success.

1. Net profit

This is always the headline that a company will produce when they report to the market and investors and the metric the media immediately reports. Yes, it is important because it helps move markets and is often one key measure that CEOs' performance bonus is based upon. If it's not clear: you subtract taxes and interest from operating income, and you are left with the net profit.

Why it's important

It's the headline figure because it's a great indicator of your company's health or distress.

Often the net profit is the number that can quickly move a company's share price on the market.

It's the key indicator used by investors on performance

2. Operating cash flow (OCF)

While net profit often grabs the headlines, this KPI shows the underlying performance of the company. It illustrates whether a company is actually making money — so keep a close eye on this metric — and for many analysts goes beyond profit. It captures the two-way movement of revenues and expenses going through the company's accounts.

One additional way analysts use this measure is to look at it against gross capital invested, to provide a better idea of return on capital.

Why it's important

It provides a quick summary of a company's money flow.

Changes in this measure can track improved or deteriorating performance in a company.

It clearly shows whether a company is tracking its revenues and spending — and answers that critical question of whether it is operating within its means.

3. Accounts payable

Maintaining strong cash flow relies on a company being able to handle what it owes and the terms of those payments. This KPI is the sum of all outstanding bills owed by the business and any short-term debts undertaken by the company. In accounting terms, this is not an asset, but a liability. It can have a significant overhang impact on the company's performance, especially if there is any disruption to revenues.

Why it's important

If a company loses track of this key accounting metric, or KPI, it won't keep up with its payments or debts.

The terms of the payments are also critical. When they have cash-flow issues companies are sometimes able to renegotiate payment terms to buy more time—but they should inform shareholders of this.

If short-term debt becomes a problem to manage, companies can refinance debt with other financial providers to reduce costs or find other forms of finance (e.g. issue stock options) to pay down debt.

4. Accounts receivable

No company survives without making money. This KPI measures the funds customers owe the business. Companies should always specify the average number of days it takes accounts receivable to be paid. Look for trends such as whether those number of days are going up or down. The best companies try to keep this number low, by encouraging customers to pay early or on time.

It is important to know that goods and services bought on credit would also be included in accounts receivable.

Why it's important

Trends in revenues will drive cash flow and profits and, as long as the company can control costs, is an important indicator of financial performance.

Controlling the size and terms of accounts receivable prevents any business from running low on cash on hand.

Watch out for how companies comment on customer payments and whether it is getting out of hand.

5. Working capital

This is another critical indicator for the health of any company. It highlights a company's cash on hand. Without having working capital, a company cannot pay all its debts. It is in fact a key measure of solvency. Cash on hand also needs to be accessible, which means it is available when a company needs it to pay its bills.

Most companies will specify cash on hand in their accounts, so it should be easy to identify, but make sure you compare this figure against any short-term debts and the maturity of those debts, and any trends in accounts payable.

Why it's important

Cash on hand is a key measure for any investor on how a company is doing to manage its funding — not just to pay its debts, but also to consider how it will finance future growth plans.

Watch out for whether account receivables are high compared to cash at hand, and growing. Remember that working capital is the financial cushion that any company has if operating conditions turn bad.

Working capital can be enhanced by short-term measures such as selling an asset, but it is watching the longer term trends of this measure that's important.

6. Cash burn rate

We've focused a lot on how companies manage their cash on hand, but this KPI is particularly important for start-up companies, which might not have ongoing strong revenues to continually build up cash reserves. Typically these companies have raised funds to create or develop a specific product and won't have income until that product is released to the market. The cash burn is the rate at which a business is eating into its cash reserves or cash balance and should be reported when it releases its accounts. Sometimes start-up companies, which attract investors by some sort of product innovation they are developing, will have to go back to investors to raise extra funds if their costs exceed their expected cash burn. That can have an impact on their share price because they are diluting shares.

Why it's important

Investors need to keep monitoring this metric closely to ensure that companies don't run out of funds and understand where their major costs are coming from.

Trends in cash burn can mean companies have to take other measures to reduce costs, such as cutting overheads or staffing costs.

Start-up companies that are forced to go back to the market to raise additional funds too often start to lose investor confidence.

7. The operating margin

This accounting measure shows investors how good a company is at generating income from running its day-to-day activities—what its margin (profit) is after costs to be able to sell its products. Investors can calculate this KPI after subtracting the cost of product, development, advertising and other business costs from its revenues.

Why do we calculate this?

This measure shows how good the company is performing at selling its products or services. Monitoring trends can illustrate if this margin is growing or squeezing depending on market conditions or changes to costs.

It helps investors understand whether they are getting a strong return from production or whether they need to do more in marketing or sales to boost revenues.

8. Return on equity (ROE)

This accounting measure illustrates if the amount of funds invested is making an adequate return. This can be critical when it comes to valuation. It compares the net income of a business to its net worth to determine whether its market value is considered fair, or above or below valuation. This is particularly important when it comes to determining whether a company's share price is considered good value.

Why it's important

ROE is a very fair predictor of the current and future worth for any company.

A positive and growing ROE can help reassure investors that the company is operating with a good net profit margin and is likely to improve its financial performance in the future.

9. Direct cost

This accounting measure is particularly important when a company might rely almost exclusively on one product or service to sell. In this case, the direct cost shows the costs associated with the manufacture, marketing or distribution of that product. In effect it shows how efficient the company is in producing that product or service.

This can also show up how competitive that company is at producing that product when considered against competitive rivals — when their direct costs are compared.

The more effective that company is at producing key products, the higher the profits. Direct costs should be kept as low as possible.

Why it's important

Investors should be aware of the input costs from creating key products and what companies are doing to keep them low, such as switching suppliers when that's possible or reducing other overheads.

This helps investors to calculate the operating margin.

10. Net promoter score (NPS)

We all know that the customer is king. This important measure charts customer satisfaction. The NPS is calculated when the company surveys its customers or has market research companies do it for them.

Companies should also be closely monitoring social media activity on their products and customer complaints. NPS is a good key performance indicator to see if a company is being valued by customers and their expectations are being met.

Companies also regularly undertake NPS measures of their employees. This is important for investors to know because unhappy or disengaged employees will have an impact on future performance through declining productivity or staff turnover, which can impact recruitment costs.

Why it's important

Investors know that sales depend on customer satisfaction, and it can also help predict customer retention for the future.

This measure helps to identify areas of strength and opportunity for any company's customer service.

Investors should also know how a company's employees feel about it and whether they are aligned to its strategy.

Choosing shares wisely

Whether you can add stocks to your investment portfolio all depends on your understanding of the company you'd like to invest in—whether it is listed or not.

Current share price

You will hear me say in this book on multiple occasions that watching the share price of a company is looking in the rear vision mirror, and we should all be more forward looking, but it is still relevant to monitor the price at which a share of stock or any other security last traded on the market.

Think of the current share price as the foundation on which to build your decision making. It's what the market is priced at on any given trade day and particular point in time. Where buyers meet sellers at any particular time is where the share price lands. Is it fair value? Well, some of the metrics outlined in this chapter will help you decide, but look for the trends—is the price moving up, down or sideways? Do investors have a strong idea of the future direction of the company? The share price, despite being a historical barometer of company performance is still an important measure to closely watch—after all if you want to buy shares in a company it will determine how much you will have to pay.

Market sentiment

We all hear a lot about something that is often described as market sentiment, which is either viewed as positive or negative. Put simply it's a group perception of the outlook of a stock, sometimes driven by media reports, sometimes driven by share price movements, and sometimes driven by broader market or consumer trends, which are likely to filter down to the company

Consider a few years ago when Buy Now Pay Later was all the rage and companies who were making zero profits were being traded at significant multiples of revenues—which throws aside all the rational metrics that investors should be considering.

In recent times, lithium stocks have been influenced by the price of lithium used in the manufacture of EV cars, which are expected to exponentially grow in market share across the globe.

Market sentiment is something that can be both good and bad for investors. It can supercharge the price of shares in a company in which you already own stock, but it can also make a stock excessively expensive to buy if investors are jumping on board the sentiment.

Sentiment can also quickly turn from positive to negative, so if you buy when the price is high you might not like it if the price suddenly drops.

It's important to closely monitor market sentiment—but don't get sucked in by it. As with everything, do your research.

Consider the company's product

The future value of a company—and its likely share price—will probably be determined mostly by the product or service it sells. First, investors should know if the company is clear about its strategy and how it will sell the product or service.

Investors should check that the company conducts adequate market research before introducing new products to determine their future market opportunities. No company operates in isolation in any marketplace, so investors should also keep an eye out for what competitors are doing with similar products or overall market trends, which could be influenced by international forces, economic changes or government regulation.

There is also a greater risk if a company only sells one product or service and hasn't diversified its income streams.

Future demand

Investors know that net profits rise and fall on supply and demand issues. Demand forecasting is difficult for investors to undertake but they should question the company at appropriate opportunities about what sort of predictive analysis they are doing to estimate and predict customers' future demand for products or services. Demand forecasting helps any business make better informed supply decisions that can help drive total sales and enhance revenue for a future period of time.

Share movements

Share price analysis is an art in its own right. There are chartists and analysts who spend hours looking at the direction in which particular prices of securities are moving. Share price movements are generally made up of peaks and troughs. This means looking at movements over a longer time frame. Generally speaking, don't buy or sell only based on the movements of these market trends (do the other research outlined in this chapter), but share movements are a key indicator of shifts in market sentiment, which as I've already outlined, can move prices in their own right.

Changing external environment

External environments affect the stock market and can have bigger or smaller impacts on certain stocks. For example, interest rate sensitive stocks, such as banks or building companies, might see their share price move more significantly from a change in official interest rates.

We all know global economic trends affect markets every day, but increasingly, other factors such as climate change or ESG (Environmental, Social and Corporate Governance) considerations are impacting investor decision making for particular stocks or across the market. It's difficult for individual investors to be across all these factors, but reading stock analysts' reports and undertaking other research to get a better idea of the likely external forces that will impact the company will help you decide whether you would like to invest.

Business processes

Business processes are critical to help keep any company focused, have the right checks and balances, and help promote the right strategy within the organisation. Increasingly, corporate governance from the board down throughout every organisation is critical, but so is the organisational structure and decision-making processes. Watch closely for the various committee reports to the boards on audit, remuneration and corporate governance. They will illustrate the ability of the company to meet shareholder expectations.

How the business evolves

No company should be stagnant. If it isn't moving forward, then competitors will overtake them. Any business needs to change to meet the needs of its customers. This requires leadership and strong board direction. Investors needs to know and see that decision making and how all business will evolve to adapt to market changes, customer trends or the broader external environment. The bigger companies have significant resources, access to research, capital and people to plan to pivot to changes in demand, and in particular, threats to the world of business. It's important for investors to know this work is going on all the time.

KEY QUESTIONS FOR INVESTORS BEFORE THEY INVEST

These are the most important questions to ask yourself before becoming a share investor in any company:

- Why am I attracted to the company?
- Have I done the right amount of research?
- Am I dedicated to attending all meetings including the AGM every year and meeting with the CEO?
- Can I easily roll off the names of the entire board and do I know their background and where they came from?

If you answered no to any of the above, you are not serious about becoming a share investor in that company.

The bottom line?

Unfortunately, most investors buy companies on the back of tips, a research house, a list of hot stocks in a share magazine or even the recommendation of a stockbroker they might know.

You have to do far more research than that.

In my experience, everyday investors often pour as much as 80 to 90 per cent of their investment allocations into the stock market at one point and hope.

Buying shares is about juggling three things:

1. *Asset allocation:* Some get this right—but you need a balanced portfolio if possible.

2. *Stock selection:* Most get this wrong—but do your research.

3. *Timing:* Almost everyone gets this wrong—don't just follow the follower.

The good news is during my 35 years of investing and assisting others to invest, I have found that asset allocation alone has saved most people over the medium to long term. I have rarely met or heard of people who got super rich by picking the timing of the market or with specific stock selection.

LET'S REFLECT ...

- Shares are an important part of any investment portfolio, but investing means following a series of important metrics.

- How good is your research and ability to study a target company for investment? You need to have resources such as time and you should invest in independent analysts' reports to help your search.

- Ensure you have an informed understanding of a company you're considering adding to your portfolio, whether the company is listed or not.

- What price the share is at now will not determine its future value: be forward looking.

- Assess market sentiment carefully: it can make or break your investment.

- Over what time frame are you prepared to hold the shares? How long can you afford to wait for any upswing or improvement in this company?

CHAPTER 5

TAX: HOW TO MANAGE AND STRUCTURE IT CORRECTLY

We all know that tax is something no-one can avoid. However, having the right tax strategy can be a game changer when it comes to building wealth.

One of the first things you must do is seek the appropriate advice on tax and develop the right structures to suit your individual circumstances.

The result will be worth it when it comes to reaching your financial goals. The aim, of course, is to lower the tax on your investments (and income where possible) so there is more money in your wallet you can use to continue to invest. The flip side—which is investing primarily for the tax advantages—is fraught with danger as many of the schemes that promote this outcome are not secure for the long term. As in life, it's all about balance.

First, it's important to understand how investment income is taxed.

It's your obligation to include investment income in your tax return. This includes anything you earn from:

- *rent*—from your investment properties

- *dividends*—from your shares

- *interest*—from fixed income securities and other forms of investment

- *distributions*—which can be anything from equity in a company to what your managed fund might pay you

- *any capital gains from property, shares and cryptocurrencies*—noting that a capital loss will also reduce your tax (more on this shortly).

You will pay tax on any investment income at your marginal rate (which is determined by your income). You can use one of the income tax calculators offered by most tax agents—and on the ATO website—to find out your marginal tax rate.

Tax deductions can be the key to reducing your tax burden. These deductions depend on the type of investment asset you own but they can involve costs associated with buying, selling or managing your investments.

If you're unsure of what tax deductions you can claim, talk to your accountant. The ATO website also lists a range of allowable investment income deductions.

In general terms, tax shouldn't intimidate or limit your investment decision making. But it can be complex, so find the right adviser to help you.

There are some key tax issues you should consider when managing your investments. We'll have a look at them now.

Superannuation

While superannuation on its own might not allow you to reach your financial retirement goals, nonetheless it remains a tax-effective investment and one of the best ways to save for retirement. This is because the government provides several tax incentives for saving through superannuation, including the following:

- You can take advantage of the tax rate of 15 per cent on all employer super contributions and salary sacrifice additional contributions of your own. The tax rate will be lower than your marginal tax rate, but it only applies if the total contribution is below the annual cap, set at $27 500 at the time of writing. When it comes to tax time, if you haven't met your annual cap, consider adding more to your super if possible—there will be benefits when you receive your tax return.

- You can make investment earnings. Remember that it's your job (whether your super fund is self-managed or not) to grow your nest egg. Earnings will also only be taxed at a rate of 15 per cent and for capital gains the tax rate is only 10 per cent.

- The ATO does not charge tax on withdrawals from super for most people over the age of 60. This has to be the greatest benefit of super. It therefore pays, as you get closer to retirement, to top up your super fund.

- When you start retirement, investment earnings become tax free if you initiate a pension paid by your super fund.

Always read your superannuation policy and closely monitor your fund's performance—be active and not passive about keeping a close eye on your superannuation.

Capital gains

All investors hope to achieve a capital gain from acquiring an investment asset when they sell it. The size of the gain depends on the price for which the investor bought the asset compared to the value they sold it for—minus any expenses or interest paid on any borrowings associated with that asset.

In Australia, any net capital gain must be included in your tax return in the financial year you sell the asset. The gain is taxed at your income (marginal) tax rate for that year. It only changes if the asset is owned within a company structure, in which case, it is taxed at a rate of 30 per cent. For self-managed super funds (SMSFs), the tax rate is 15 per cent.

One thing to remember is that it pays to hold an asset for more than 12 months to earn a capital gains tax (CGT) discount: after 12 months, you're only taxed on *half* the capital gains tax.

If you're unsure, consult your accountant—and, again, there is plenty of information on CGT tax rates on the ATO website.

Remember to keep all relevant information when lodging your tax return, including your purchase and sales receipts.

Capital losses

Not all investment assets are sold at a profit. Sometimes investors have no option but to sell and sometimes it's better to offload an underperforming asset to offset capital gain that might have been earned from the sale of other assets. If you make a capital loss, you must declare it in the financial year in which the asset was sold — with the advantage that it may offset other tax obligations, at your marginal tax rate.

The other tax advantage of a capital loss, apart from reducing other capital gains, is that it is possible to carry forward the loss to offset future capital gains.

HOW CAPITAL LOSS WORKS

Jane bought a bundle of 50 speculative shares at $40 each — spending $2000 in total.

She gradually saw the shares fall in value and after 18 months decided to cut her losses and sell the shares. At that stage they were worth $20 each — in other words, they had halved in value. As a result, Jane had made a capital loss of $1000.

The good news for Jane is she'd also made a capital gain of $1500 in the same financial year from selling some blue-chip stocks that she'd held for more than four years.

This allowed Jane to deduct the $1000 loss she'd made on her speculative stocks from the $1500 profit she'd made selling her blue-chip shares. In net terms that means Jane only had to declare a $500 capital gain.

However, since she'd held the blue-chip shares for more than 12 months, she was also able to halve the capital gain on her tax return to just $250. This gain would be taxed at her marginal tax rate in that financial year.

Positive vs negative gearing

Positive gearing and negative gearing describe two different financial incentives for investors. Be sure to understand your gears.

Positive gearing

When an investor engages in positive gearing the income earned from owning an asset (which on an investment property mostly includes rent or could be dividends from a large parcel of shares) is more than the costs associated with managing that investment (including maintaining an investment property or any interest costs associated with a loan on the asset).

This is often the case where an investor might own an investment property but only has a small mortgage on that property.

For the investor, these funds become another source of taxable income that needs to be declared to the ATO in the relevant financial year and will be taxed at the marginal tax rate.

Negative gearing

We hear a lot in Australia about negative gearing. It is tax effective if you are buying, for example, an investment property. Negative gearing is when the costs associated with managing the investment (the interest bills on the loan and the cost of maintaining the property) are less than the income derived from the investment, which in property terms is generally the rent.

This is attractive because a loan (gearing) allows the investor to buy the investment property, the rent pays for most of the loan and they can generally claim a tax deduction for the losses associated with the gap between the income and the costs from owning the investment.

Why has this become popular? Because investors can achieve an overall tax benefit and, after all, the aim of buying an investment property is to hopefully see it achieve significant capital gain by the time it is sold—which is where an investor can achieve a big increase in wealth.

Remember, if your investment income isn't covering your costs (allowing you to claim a loss), you still need income from elsewhere to meet your obligations.

Most investors who choose this way of investing have a salary or other forms of investment income to pay the bank for the investment loan.

Tax-effective investments

When we see our accountant at the end of each financial year, one of our aims is to reduce our marginal tax rate. We should all pay the tax we are legally obligated to pay, but there are ways (such as negative gearing or incurring a capital gains loss) in which the tax treatment of your investment income can impact your marginal tax rate.

Always beware of tax-driven schemes promising tax deductions now for investing in assets that may provide income in the future. These schemes can be high risk, and quite frankly some are scams. Chat with your accountant first before investing and always check the ATO website, which lists tax-avoidance schemes to avoid.

Never enter into a tax-driven investment without professional guidance.

Insurance and investment bonds

Sometimes investors are drawn to long-term investments offered by insurance—or other—companies, usually offering higher than normal returns. These are called insurance or investment bonds. Investors are often bound by certain rules about when they can cash in their bonds during the term of the investment.

It is important to know that all earnings in an investment bond are taxed at the corporate tax rate of 30 per cent, which of course might be attractive to investors with a higher marginal tax rate than 30 per cent. Important to note is that there are tax advantages if no withdrawals are made in the first 10 years.

Investment income on your tax return

Investment income must be declared each year, like all other forms of income. Investors need to keep good records and be honest about their investment income. At the same time, it is possible to reduce your tax liability on investment income by claiming all allowable deductions and being sure to accurately determine whether you have cumulatively made a capital gain or loss on the disposal of any investment asset each financial year.

For all investments—such as shares, property and crypto-currencies—you need to keep records, including:

- receipts—including a contract of sale stating how much you paid for the asset and a contract of sale stating how much you sold the asset for

- a detailed breakdown of all the income you received from the investment asset — keep all the dividend distribution statements you have received from listed companies, rental payment receipts from your tenants and any other income statements

- a detailed breakdown of any expenses paid as the owner of the investment asset — which can include receipts to maintain an investment property for payments and any other expenses to manage or improve the value of the asset.

I'm sure you have a better filing system than a shoe box, so don't forget you need to keep these financial records for five years, even after you've declared the income or capital gain or loss in your current financial year.

***

Don't get flustered by tax even though it seems complicated and is subject to change by the government — it's a necessary evil. So make it work for you and choose the most effective tax structure you can to help you achieve your goals.

LET'S REFLECT ...

- Getting your tax structure right is critical for maximising your returns and gaining wealth.

- Get great advice, do the work to ensure you keep and maintain all the appropriate paperwork, and take advantage of capital gains and capital losses.

- As with a capital gain, if you make a capital loss, you must declare it in the financial year in which the asset was sold.

- Superannuation is a tax-effective investment and one of the best ways to save for retirement. Be active, not passive, about keeping a close eye on your super.

- Do not be driven only by tax-advantageous investments as these schemes typically attract higher risk and can be scams. Always check the ATO website, which lists tax-avoidance schemes, and never enter into a tax-driven investment without professional guidance.

- You need to keep financial records for five years, even after you've declared the income or capital gain or loss in your current financial year.

- Do not be intimated by tax: the proper structure can reduce your marginal tax rate.

CHAPTER <u>6</u>

LEVERAGE: ADVANCED INSTRUMENTS FOR BUILDING WEALTH

There's an old saying: 'Money is a bit like soap: the more you play with it, the less you have'.

Any successful investor or business owner needs the right information to make the right decisions. That's becoming harder because there is so much content out there that you could spend all your time just researching. To make it easier, I'll share with you some of the books that I believe any investor should devour, and touch on the philosophies of some remarkable world-renowned leaders who have assisted others.

The books include:

- *Think and grow rich* by Napoleon Hill

- *The millionaire next door* by Thomas J Stanley and William D Danko

- *Rich dad, poor dad* by Robert Kiyosaki and Sharon Lechter

- *Money: master the game* by Tony Robbins

- *Principles* by Ray Dalio.

These resources have helped me create the rationale, clarity and practical steps for financial independence.

Understanding investment instruments

You need to be clear about and to understand what you're doing before you start any financial plan.

Before you read about the big picture (in part II of this book), first you must understand the instruments that any investor should be able to use. For example, an understanding of hedging is mandatory, as well as taking out the right insurance for your investments. Keep coming back to the following definitions as you continue to progress through this book because the average Western world investor shouldn't sweat on the market only going one way.

Cash instruments

These are in common use. We obtain cash instruments almost daily when we trade on the market or interact with our bank or other financial institutions. Market conditions such as interest rate movements and price changes impact their value. Generally they fall into two types: securities and loans/deposits:

- *Securities:* Shares can come in many different forms, and are most often traded on the stock market. When we buy a security we generally own a share in something wider that we can trade depending on its value and the demand of a buyer.

- *Loans/deposits:* Almost every Australian has a deposit account at their bank, but we buy fixed-interest deposit products as part of our savings for retirement plans. Most Australians will also take out a loan at some stage of their life, whether that's for a home, car or to buy the latest widescreen TV. To obtain a loan requires a contractual agreement between parties.

Who's likely to use them?

Retail and private investors frequently use these types of exchange-listed or bank-issued securities and that's because they are readily available and priced daily. They are available via investment platforms of various types all over the world.

Pros

Securities such as shares offer investors the opportunity to buy into the performance of a company. We know most securities offer a high level of accessibility and liquidity so investors can decide when they will buy and sell.

Deposits are more stable, generally offering monthly or yearly returns and quarterly and yearly fixed rates of return. Loans are a critical way for investors to leverage effectively to grow their investment portfolio.

Cons

When you trade anything on a market as an investor you are subject to market swings that are sometimes beyond your control. Smaller retail investors also have smaller amounts to invest than larger institutional investors, so they will only benefit from smaller returns.

Both deposits and loans are subject to interest-rate movements; these needs to be anticipated as can hurt investors.

While deposits are generally protected by bank guarantees, their returns can be low and rarely offer a hedge against inflation over the longer term.

Derivative instruments

Derivative instruments are different from cash instruments because their value is determined by movements in the asset in which you invest. For example, an investor might take a position on how base metal prices such as copper might move or on the value of currencies, bonds or stocks and even stock indexes. These forms of investment are usually undertaken by institutional investors, but for sophisticated retail investors they can also offer opportunities. What this means is the investor is in financial instruments that have values determined from underlying assets such as resources, currency, bonds, stocks and stock indexes.

There are a range of derivative instruments, but the five most common examples are options, swaps, forwards, futures and a broad term known as synthetic agreements:

- *Options* are agreements between two parties to buy and sell a product at a pre-determined price for a specific period.

- *Forwards* are where the transaction occurs at an agreed price at the end of a contract.

- *Futures* are contracts to buy and sell at a determined date and exchange rate.

- *Swaps* are less common among retail investors. These are mostly interest-rate swaps where each party agrees to the other's interest rates, sometimes even in a different currency.

- *Synthetic agreements* have their exchange and lock in a specific exchange rate for a period of time. That's mostly important for big companies undertaking large contracts in international currencies who are worried about exchange-rate movements.

Who's likely to use them?

A large investor wanting to add additional leverage to their portfolio or position in a particular company is likely to use these. Often these instruments are used to protect an investor's position in case of changes to market conditions such as interest-rate movements or currency shifts. Options can help investors purchase shares in a company for a fraction of the cost of the share.

Pros

These types of derivatives can help investors fast track their investment portfolios because for a smaller outlay they can own options in shares rather than having to buy the physical shares.

If they understand the market, these derivatives can help investors protect their investment.

Once you've done the research, they aren't difficult markets to trade.

Cons

Derivative instruments can involve higher risks than cash instruments. When you own a cash instrument you own the security and you can still sell it even if it falls in value. If you trade a derivative and the market turns against you, then that derivative might become worthless or, even worse, the cost of the transaction can be more than you paid for it at settlement. That's when you can actually lose money.

There is likely to be less liquidity in this market compared to cash instruments, meaning it is harder to buy and sell. There is also more risk from external factors impacting the market. For example, commodity prices might be impacted by drought, climate change or shifts in economic conditions.

Foreign exchange instruments

The foreign exchange market has developed its own instruments, which primarily help traders manage changes in currencies, mostly on behalf of large investors or companies. Retail investors usually don't use these instruments, but all investors should be aware of their existence, especially when they are monitoring their superannuation funds or investment funds, which are likely to use them.

Among these instruments there are terms we have all heard, such as 'spot trading' (an agreement to buy and sell currency no later than the second working day from when the agreement is reached) and 'forwards' (the same thing, done now but for an agreed forward date). Then there is also what's known as a 'currency swap'—which is a bit more complicated—where different currencies are bought and sold at agreed dates and values.

Who's likely to use them?

These types of derivatives are generally used by trading businesses (sometimes working on behalf of companies) or large investors wanting to lock in currency prices and protect their position today for a time of transaction in the future. They offer peace of mind and security to enhance business management. For example, a company that has a large order for steel in six months can lock in the price and the terms of the currency exchange now in case the price of steel jumps in the interim.

Pros

Investors reap the benefits of greater security by only paying a small premium, depending on market pricing, to lock in currency pricing now and to protect the buying and/or selling position of a product or a commodity.

Cons

Generally these types of derivatives work best for short-term trades (mainly weeks or months) where the market trends might be more realistic to predict. It's much more difficult to know where currency movements will be in six months or a year and traders who get caught on the wrong side of a currency movement can be locked into contracts that lose them money.

Instruments by asset class

There is another way of differentiating more sophisticated investment instruments and that's by asset class.

Generally speaking, these are separated into debt-based financial instruments and equity-based financial instruments. The pathway that investors choose to take for one or both of these instruments can have significant implications.

Debt-based financial instruments

When you need to raise funds for investment purposes, or if you own your own business and need capital to grow or acquire another business, you often look to debt. Companies can issue bonds or other mechanisms such as debentures, which don't diminish their owner's stake, to do this. However, for individuals, raising funds can be anything from taking out a mortgage, a loan against the business or even in extreme circumstances using your credit card. Debt shouldn't be something investors are afraid to embrace — but remember it comes with interest and a repayment schedule that you must have the cash flow to meet.

Who's likely to use them?

Debt-based instruments such as bonds and debentures are usually issued or bought by businesses, either listed or unlisted. Of course they are also available to small-to-medium-sized businesses and individual investors. They can assist growth in a business expansion phase in the areas of capital, equipment and human resources — in fact, in almost anything that is required for the business operation and expansion.

Pros

Debt-based instruments sometimes offer finance at a fixed cost for a fixed term that can be budgeted to manage. The advantage is they won't diminish the ownership structure, which means giving away any of the upside for operational or long-term growth in the business enterprise. Often an emerging business will take on debt before paying it down when it lists on the stock market and raises funds in other ways.

Individuals who can manage debt repayments can leverage their investment portfolio, enabling them to take a more significant stake in an attractive investment.

Cons

Investors buying debt-based instruments in a company or fund will only ever receive a fixed rate of return that is binding over a specified term from those instruments, meaning they have no entitlements to growth or upside in the business valuation. Unlike being a stockholder, these investors also have no control over the performance of the business.

Equity-based financial instruments

These instruments don't cost the individual or business anything upfront (it's more like paying interest on a loan), but they do diminish the ownership structure of the entity issuing them.

These types of instruments are mostly used by business when they issue stocks, rights or convertible debentures. Individuals might use them to access equity in a major asset they own, such as their home, or to raise funds for something such as aged care.

Who's likely to use them?

Investors who buy an equity-based financial instrument mostly have the option to sell it later—just ensure there is plenty of liquidity in the asset you purchase so you can buy and sell whenever you wish.

Equity-based instruments are mainly used for listed and unlisted companies. Sometimes smaller or medium enterprise investors use equity-based instruments for their expansion when they incur additional unexpected operational costs or with the purpose of financing growth and expansion of the services or products they provide. Equity-based instruments are very good for encouraging investors to come along the journey in the medium to long term. Assuming success, all parties in the future enjoy the fruits of the growth of the business, providing of course they can sell its products or services.

Pros

Equity-based instruments are great instruments for offering investors access to the ownership of legal entitlement to the company itself, which may entitle them to income (dividends), any capital growth and in some cases a say (via voting) on the direction of the business.

Cons

Investors taking only a small portion of an equity-based instrument in a company or fund ultimately have no control over that entity, and its performance remains at the behest of the CEO and senior management.

Equity-based instruments offer no guarantee of distribution income, no guarantee of capital growth, no guarantee of a return on their investment nor a guaranteed return of their investment.

The returns for equity investors are predicated on the substance of management direction delivering on products and services and having the systems in place to create the returns.

***

Collectively, using these instruments effectively can be very powerful in building wealth—they add to your leveraging toolkit—but make sure you know what you're doing and don't lose control. I have never relied on something I have no control over to achieve the outcomes I'm seeking in my business life and those who know me best say it's my strongest trait: control the strategy.

I invest in stock markets and use some of these instruments, but I'll also tell you I learned a hell of a lot about hedging and insurance (both covered in this book) when I was in my early 20s and I use these principles in almost every aspect of my life when making business and life decisions. In the end, the market conditions will usually provide you with assistance as to which path to take or not.

Debt or equity for growth will always be priced differently in changing markets. Today, at the time of writing, I would say that debt-based instruments are better for investors right now due to current pricing and offerings. This, of course, assumes you have a terrific company and fantastic cash flows. Hold onto as much equity as possible until you go public because control is everything in achieving the outcomes you are seeking.

LET'S REFLECT ...

- There are plenty of great books about leveraging instruments that you can read and they are a great resource, but you also need to understand the instruments that are available to help you leverage.

- Advanced leveraging isn't for everyone, but for different investors and asset classes it can be incredibly helpful.

- Loans are a critical way for investors to leverage effectively to grow their investment portfolio.

- Any successful investor or business owner needs the right information to make the right decisions.

- Most important is to understand the instruments that investors should be able to use, in particular hedging.

- Only use these advanced instruments if you know what you're doing or have expert help.

- Collectively, advanced leveraging instruments can be very powerful wealth builders to add to your leveraging toolkit, but ensure you stay in control and follow a strategy.

PART I: KEY TAKEAWAYS

- Leveraging takes many forms and when combined these can supercharge your wealth opportunities.

- Change your mindset, especially over retirement planning. You must take control.

- Traditional forms of wealth creation such as property and shares offer great opportunities, even though the environment in which they operate is rapidly changing.

PART II

LEVERAGING TOOLS AND APPROACHES

CHAPTER 7

TIME, MONEY, ENERGY AND PEOPLE: LEVERAGE YOUR RESOURCES

Intelligent leverage isn't only about borrowing money. It's also about your ability to produce the outcomes you're seeking by leveraging all the resources you have at your disposal.

Most adults today wouldn't give a second thought, or a first one for that matter, to the ability to track progress, analyse status and seek solutions where impediments arise. Every day, on each business project I'm involved in, I consider the end value I'm looking to maximise through financial feasibility reports, and I review the bottom-line outcome I'm aiming to achieve at the completion of each project. I've found that you can accurately forecast up to around 98 per cent.

The alternative is wishful thinking, which is as much as most people hope to achieve. It's like everybody wants to go to heaven, but no-one wants to die.

This leads to fear and a reliance on hope. I have a saying for that: 'Hope is for the hopeless'. Most people aren't disciplined enough, or don't possess the knowledge, to understand that building anything from real wealth—a business, a building or the right mentoring relationships—takes an exchange of time, deep analysis and a lot of energy.

When fear is present and leaders retreat into their shell, the call on knowledge is distorted because they don't want to know the reality or can't process it. Conversely, when knowledge and capabilities are high, fear shrivels into oblivion.

For more than 35 years I've observed people seek to materialise their investment dream and pray for it to be an easy and pleasant journey. This quest for a wonderfully peaceful, stress-free and joyful path generally stems from a lack of understanding and comprehension around the effort achieving their purpose and desired outcome requires.

Get your focus right

Your aim should be to think of yourself as your own corporation and focus on and understand what you are good, or even great, at doing. We all have strengths and weaknesses.

I'm fortunate enough to know that I'm a thinker, creatively orientated, a good communicator and I can motivate others. That's largely because I'm self-motivated. What I don't enjoy is working through boring administrative procedures and processes even though they are important elements of any business project.

That's not to say I don't get the required paperwork done. I accept that it's a mandatory process and a key requirement to achieving the final goal or outcome. What I have done is build a team around me that assists me in achieving that end goal, to ensure that it is carried out and completed. I know I need help sometimes on the detail and so I make sure I ask for help.

We can't all employ a team, but paying a part-time bookkeeper, or touching base with your financial planner as required, can help enormously to keep you cash-flow positive. Without a foundation, a structure and processes your efforts will be fruitless. It's like building a car without a manual or design guidelines.

That's intelligent leverage. Of course, the reverse is also true. I know thousands of managers and people who understand procedures and processes, but who will never become financially independent because they aren't imaginative enough, can't leverage their vocation or don't have the required personal exertion. For these people it's about networking to find creative people or investing in time to grow their wealth or business.

It's the combination of having an idea and then implementing it that matters.

We all have the same 24 hours in the day to achieve outcomes; it's what we do with that time that makes the difference. The inventiveness and creativity of an individual is what sets them apart in many aspects of life.

I understand that we can only utilise the skills we are born with. However, we can enhance those skills by spending time analysing a project thoroughly, searching for ideas that will spark a brilliant vision or solution, or reaching out to someone in the industry—without giving away your IP of course.

If you're focused on the big picture, there are people who can be paid to help produce policy or craft a procedures manual.

Build economic success

In general terms, there are five mechanics to economic success:

1. access to capital

2. the right systems

3. innovative management

4. product differentiation

5. effective distribution.

Business wealth and success are a combination of these mechanics and they embrace the intellectual operational hub. You must never stop thinking about how to differentiate what you do and adapt to change.

I compare this process to restoring classic cars, which is one of my great loves. It involves working with the engine, chassis, steering, brakes, suspension and wiring as well as making it look presentable with new paint and a revamped interior.

It might help you visualise what needs to be done if you think about it in terms of building a classic car. The elements are all there:

- *Chassis:* structure, framework and foundation

- *Motor:* product sales and distribution capacity

- *Suspension:* people, culture and capital adequacy

- *Agility:* product improvement and communication to clients

- *Systems:* process and procedures

- *Braking:* compliance, governance and warning signals

- *Lighting:* ability to see into the future.

- *Interior:* feel, culture and experience

- *Exterior:* social acceptance, trust and credibility

- *Badging:* brand, trust and credibility.

When I decided to focus on global high-net-worth customers, I built business relationships that reach far beyond just the financial. We understand each other in almost a telepathic way, and we feed off each other. That's how you should become with your key customers: anticipate their needs and offer solutions before they need them.

Scale isn't everything

When I started my accountancy and financial planning business it wasn't long before I had more than 30000 clients, with a team of advisers helping these clients with financial matters, wealth-creation planning, estate protection and taxation planning. In other words, 'make it soundly and keep it'. But I remember at the age of 45 I realised that while I had built my business to a substantial scale, it felt distinctly empty, and I had few meaningful relationships with any of my clients. I couldn't help them build real wealth.

So, I did something about it. I made the commitment to myself that I would transfer all of my clients—except for a key 25—to my company adviser employees as we had the resources to provide better services and outcomes for this very large clientele, and direct my energy and attention to only building a maximum manageable number of 100 ultra-high-net-worth clients.

This was a group I knew I would be able to maintain to the standard that was required, and I wanted to be with those people because I loved working with them. Today I work with around 68 high-net-worth families from all over the world and 12 ultra-high-net-worth individuals. This list will never exceed 100. This group has come together because we have mutual interests and investment outlooks, but the outcomes are very much performance driven.

The 'definiteness of purpose' (as Napoleon Hill puts it) is that I work in a collaborative way in perfect harmony with these clients. We pool our ideas, time, energy and of course resources for the best example of intelligent leverage I can think of. The result is that I manage around $21 billion in funds globally, which can be directed in ways to achieve goals across the group. And I'm happier than I've ever been in my life. The laws of attraction were at work when I wanted scale, scale, scale, but I took control over what type of scale would work best and now have intelligent leverage at work.

It's like a scene from a movie

After moving on from a small boy wanting to become an astronaut (only to be told that would mean I would have to move to the United States as there was no space program in Australia), I took an interest in acting. Going to the movies was a great reprieve from study, and the endless amount of reading and homework.

So, when I was a young teenager, I attended the Australian Academy of Media in Melbourne twice a week to hone my acting skills. One day, after about three months, I realised that I didn't have the time required, nor the patience, to make it as an actor.

I accepted the remote chance of success and changed my mind. It was a turning point. This led me straight back to what I was good at in school, which was mathematics. In short, logic kicked in early for me, as the risks were way too high for me to rely on hope.

Why am I mentioning this?

Today, when I undertake a project, I think of it as like working on a movie set. My love of movies is relatable to what I do every day. It all takes place in a series of scenes (the actions), it must have a location (the where), the actors (who/the people), the mission or work (theme/story) and I need to be the director/producer (find the finance) and editor (change the scenes around to make them work) of what I do in my life.

In short, success in life is about creating a wonderful movie scene.

That requires constant action. If I hear about people aspiring for 'passive income' one more time I'll scream!

The term 'passive'; in relation to income is misleading and deceptive. It's like saying to someone that you want to be 'passive' when it comes to your health or your marriage or the most important relationships in your life. It just doesn't work over time.

As I said, intelligent leverage comes in many forms, not just the obvious, which is borrowing money against assets. Understanding the breadth of what leverage can achieve is probably the most powerful concept for anyone wanting to succeed in business or in the investment world. You must control the structure and platform of your asset base and build the right networks and ecosystem to catapult you into the next stratosphere towards financial independence. The knock-on effect and outcomes will include the ability to help others because you become a mentor for others. It's a virtuous circle when it works out.

The stress factor

What's the best use of your time in today's world of advanced technology? Technology has helped everyone enormously over the past 50 years, enabling us to do more with less. However, current research indicates that we endure more frustration, stress and anxiety than at any other time over the past 100 years and that financial independence has not improved—it has actually regressed.

Everyone experiences stress. We all experience different types of stress levels, and it seems, on the surface at least, that some people can cope with it better than others. Those who can't, quickly learn mechanisms to help them cope—if they recognise the issue.

I'm not a psychologist so it's not my place to list the causes of stress, but we know that today's fast-paced lifestyle, with everyone staying connected via social media on their smartphones is probably making it worse.

The Australian Psychological Society (APS) produced a report in 2015 that would still be relevant today. The report was based on a survey that found Australians are faring worse than they were in 2011, which was the previous time the APS conducted a survey.

The report found that about one-third of Australians have significant levels of distress in their lives and in 2015 anxiety symptoms were the highest they had been since the previous survey was conducted five years prior the report.

The report, not surprisingly, found that personal finance was the top cause of stress. This was true for half of the people surveyed. Unremarkably, personal health wasn't that far behind, with 44 per cent of people nominating it as a major cause of anxiety.

Social media was seen as both a cause and a way of managing stress. In a worrying trend of Australia's next working generation, one outcome of the survey was that one-quarter of all teenagers reported using social media every day when they were eating breakfast or lunch.

Our lifestyle and environmental factors are clearly adding to our stress, and we are most concerned about our personal financial situation. There are more distractions and pressures to match the spending habits of others, who show off on Instagram or other platforms. It seems we need instant shopping gratification and that is precisely the reason why most will never make or win the financial independence end game.

We need to stop buying junk we don't need at so-called irresistible prices. Of course, I haven't been immune or totally disciplined about avoiding shopping temptations either, but now, in my 50s, and given the world is in the most concerning state for decades, I've changed my mindset to only try and buy what I need, as opposed to what I want.

Discipline in an age of constant distractions is grossly underestimated.

LET'S REFLECT ...

- Intelligent leverage comes in many forms, not only as a way to borrow money. The goal is to leverage all the resources you have at your disposal—not only the financial ones.

- Focus on the big picture and tap into your resources to build a solid network around you.

- Hope is for the hopeless: think about how you should leverage your time and contacts to be proactive.

- Work out how to bring all the elements together, as if you were restoring a classic car.

- Consider making your outcomes performance driven, not scale driven, so that you can give your utmost attention to all of your clients.

- Discipline and not giving in to technological distractions can give you a flying start.

CHAPTER <u>8</u>

FINANCIAL SUCCESS: IT STARTS WITH YOU

The most fundamental asset you have in your life is, of course, you. That means it's essential to invest in your mental, physical, emotional and spiritual health. They are as important as financial health. Without these, you can't achieve your broader goals. And meditation and sleep can't be taken for granted—just ask the top 1 per cent of income earners on the planet who swear by wellness.

In the 1980s and 1990s, thanks to the media and legendary stories of rockstar CEOs, the image of a successful businessperson was projected as a big, loud, back-slapping person encompassing a 'she'll be right mate' attitude. They were the ones to grab the microphone at an event or order another glass of wine over lunch. These were the fast-talking, cigar-smoking Gordon Gekko types, who could knock down a few whiskies during the day and plough through work to still make the big bucks.

If the almost 99 per cent of my personal networks and successful associates and friends are any guide, the business leaders and serious investors of today are more conscious of the importance of sleep, diet and exercise to promote longevity and good health for maximum performance in this competitive world.

Some of my close business associates have a routine—yearly, and even in some cases half-yearly—of committing to blood tests and extensive medical check-ups to feel assured that they are in good physical health.

A generation ago, some of the smartest people I've met in business didn't make it to 55 years of age often because they were thrown an unexpected curve ball on their health outlook. Blood tests, and now even saliva tests, can determine most life-threatening illnesses to watch out for and how to create a prevention regime early in life. What's the point of amassing a fortune to drop dead just over halfway through your mortality expectation?

A new era of work ethic

Remember, competition is even more fierce today than it was in the long-lunch era of the early 1980s. Back then they didn't have a thing called the internet. Today we're all expected, via our smartphone, to be constantly switched on, and consequently we're bombarded by the endless daily development of information.

Two things happened in 2007: the iPhone was launched by Apple, bringing in the era of the smartphone—which has changed how we can communicate with anyone, anywhere—and a little-known show called *Keeping up with the Kardashians* premiered on the E! channel in the United States.

For the first time ever, that show created an entire alternative world anchored in social media. It was able to monetise its commercial connections through millions of aspirational followers around the world. Yes, it got an audience on TV, but its following on social media was far more powerful. It was innovative and the content was carefully tailored. It knew what its audience wanted and it delivered.

While it was a team effort, much of the credit for *Keeping up with the Kardashians* goes to 'momager' Kris Jenner. She has been quoted as saying that there is a simple reason why the family has been so successful: determination and hard work. 'There's a lot of people that have great ideas and dreams and whatnot, but unless you're willing to work really, really hard, and work for what you want it's never going to happen,' Jenner told the *New York Times* in 2015. 'That's what's so great about the girls. It's all about their work ethic'.

The good news is that today there are so many more avenues available to reach your end goals. Previously you had to convince big investors, corporations or newspaper editors you had a good idea, whereas now you can go direct to the source, perhaps by crowdfunding or creating some content on a YouTube channel to tell people what you're doing. You can also directly connect with, or at least follow, great mentors via LinkedIn and other platforms. Yes, the information can be buried under a flood of other activity, but if you know where to look the connections are there to leverage.

Embrace the Pareto principle

The Pareto principle was created by management consultant Joseph Juran and economist Vilfredo Pareto. It's often referred to as the 80/20 rule — in other words, 80 per cent of the consequences of life come from the vital 20 per cent of causes. What does this mean? Set parameters for the things you can achieve most effectively and focus on them.

We know that successful people generally work long hours and that's especially true for those starting a business or juggling normal working hours as an employee with working on their own business project out of hours.

That's clearly necessary in the short term for many entrepreneurs, who still need to pay the household bills, but it's unsustainable in the longer term and can generate burnout and negatively impact your health.

It's better to focus on the key things that can make a difference to meeting your financial goals. That might be 20 things, or it might only be five things, depending on what's important to you.

What we're looking for is what will achieve the highest returns. If it's managing an investment portfolio and doing all the necessary research on which stocks to buy, don't try to do that for 50 stocks. Focus on those you know most about.

Of course the 80/20 rule applies to other parts of your life as well, hopefully freeing up more of your time to focus on the things that matter.

Devoting time to family and important relationships should always rank highly in your priorities, but playing that extra round of golf on the weekend or agreeing to a meeting or a drink with someone who might be marginal to your personal life goals might be questionable.

Health is another priority—and this means exercising. In my experience if you don't complete your exercise early in the day, other events will take over your diary. In addition, an early morning run or walk is a great way to clear your head and plan your day in your mind while your body is moving.

Prioritising obviously also includes managing your investments and de-stressing the process. When you're unsure, it's okay to be boring in your investments and choose to do nothing rather than constantly moving your money around. Your investment in business and capital accumulation must be constantly measured over time.

In a variation of the Pareto principle, I also largely adhere to the laws of the 80/20 benchmark when it comes to investing—which means only having 20 per cent of my capital in riskier investments.

Right now (in mid 2023, as I write this book) I have a tolerance for boredom and patience, which means doing nothing in an uncertain market. This will probably provide the best outcome financially as the market might continue to drop. Most people are selling diminishing assets to prevent even further losses, but are they thinking with their head or their heart?

The bottom line is we all need to do more with less by being more resourceful—it comes down to priorities and focus.

There comes a time when you realise that procrastination is expensive: when you look out how much time you have left and how much you have wasted. Time is finite. I've always lived by the mantra that I use every day to enhance the quality and possible length of my life. Failure is not an option.

HOW TO DO MORE WITH LESS TIME

A lot of people talk about time management, but it's another thing to make time work in your favour. I guess we've all reflected at the end of another exhausting week how things might have been done differently.

To begin with, you need to realise that there is a pathway to being more efficient in the way you use your time. I follow the steps of leading life and business coach Tony Robbins, whom I've had the pleasure of meeting.

Here are some tips based on his philosophy:

- *It's okay to say no:* no-one likes to disappoint others, but we need to be careful about committing time to meetings that we know won't help us achieve our goals, or social occasions that take up precious evening or weekend hours.

- *Change the way you work:* put aside some time to complete critical tasks. Stop checking and responding to your emails continually and don't allow yourself to get caught up in endless meetings. A quick phone conversation is sometimes all you need to sort out a situation.

- *Block tasks together:* Tony Robbins calls this 'chunking', and it can be a very powerful tool. By blocking tasks together you can kill a few birds with one stone. This avoids the usual stop–start nature of getting through your priorities. And it extends to all aspects of your life—for example, batch cooking meals on a Sunday for the whole week.

- *Plan ahead:* write your priorities down on lists along with what motivates you. Tony Robbins calls this the 'Rapid Planning Method'. It helps clear away the clutter and gives you a reference point to return to.

- *Know your purpose:* it's much easier to achieve your goals and keep knocking over your priority list if you know you're building towards something important in your life. Keep reminding yourself of what that end goal (or goals) is to help keep the motivation going.

- *Utilise your relationships and lean on experience:* you can't achieve everything on your own. There are always people who have been on the same pathway as you: try reaching out to them and checking in on your progress. Experience is a wonderful thing, so find a mentor if possible. Remember these are the relationships that will help you achieve your goals, so they are worth the investment of time and energy. It doesn't always need to be a formal encounter: it could be someone you've met in your riding or running group; it could be a neighbour; or it might be a five-minute unexpected conversation that helps crystallise your thinking.

- *Make a start and you'll get the momentum:* if you've always wanted to create an investment fund for yourself or your children, but think you've got to accumulate a substantial pool of money to make it work, think again. Start with $500 and build on it each month. You'll be surprised when you look back after six months how far you've come. Procrastination is the killer of all achievement.

Sometimes it's not just about writing lists or notes, but also carrying them around with you as a motivational tool.

(continued)

This could simply be a list of what you want to achieve that week or month.

These signposts are the important things in your life right now. It's like carrying dollar coins or 10-cent coins in your pocket. The minor (10-cent coins) things won't matter tomorrow—they just take up space in your pocket. You won't achieve all these petty, so-called must-do items anyway and if you do, I bet you'll have also lost valuable time on tasks that won't change your and your family's life in a significant way. It's better to concentrate on the dollar coins.

Goal setting creates leverage

Every action must start with a goal. Everyone talks about goals but few actually act on them. I believe in being ambitious because it forces you to act. For that reason, I set myself 20 goals that I think are critical each year.

It isn't just about setting goals, but breaking them down to reduce anxiety with the aim of avoiding blind spots, ego, excessive optimism and unexamined assumptions. In finance, this means setting realistic goals that are mostly based on asset building. Put them to a team, whether that's your partner or mentor, for real self-analysis.

One way of doing this is to start with short-term goals—don't try to be too ambitious. Once you've knocked them over you can start to move towards larger, longer term goals. It's a stepping up process.

The empowering thing about goal setting is it makes you feel like you're in control, especially if positive outcomes follow.

It's also about being true to yourself—whether that's about your investment intentions, how to turbocharge your career or just how to invest more time and energy into your relationship. Importantly, it could be all three, but it all starts with setting achievable goals. You'll make mistakes and you won't achieve all your goals, and that's okay—at least you're not giving up and you're trying to be better.

TEN ACHIEVABLE GOALS TO SET FOR YOURSELF

When setting goals for yourself, you may choose to follow the SMART goal method. This method was created by three management gurus—George Doran, Arthur Miller and James Cunningham—who in 1981 wrote an article: 'There's a SMART way to write management's goals and objectives'.

The acronym 'SMART' refers to setting Specific, Measurable, Achievable, Relevant and Time-bound objectives. These reference points could be put next to each of your major goals in a box-ticking exercise.

Here are some techniques to help you both set your goals and achieve them—and they might sound obvious, but it's amazing how few people consider them.

1. *Start by understanding yourself:* where are your skills and weaknesses? Given the pressures and other challenges in your life, what is achievable and how can you achieve your goals? What's the best place for you to work to achieve your outcomes? Most importantly, are you committed to change? This partly starts by having an open mind and accepting that mistakes will

(continued)

be made along the way. It also means acknowledging you can't achieve everything at once and understanding what you already have—whether that's family or friends—and the skills you've already exhibited. Have the confidence to know you can do this.

2. *Always be proactive:* if you don't make a start, you won't get anywhere. If you've had a setback in meeting a goal it's also natural to want to stop—but keep persevering. Yes, it's fine to re-evaluate a goal if it isn't working—and it could mean taking a short break from pursuing your goals while you do that analysis—but just keep moving forward.

3. *Be courageous enough to make the decisions:* eventually, to make change you will have to make a decision, whether that's starting an investment portfolio, changing your job, buying a new house or using the equity in your house to help refinance your small business. Yes, that takes courage, but if you've done the right research and consulted the right people, then it's time to make that move.

4. *Find ways to reduce your stress and live within your values:* making changes in your life or embarking on something new can be stressful. The most important thing is to make sure the significant people in your life, such as your family and friends, know what changes you're making and support you. This can not only keep you motivated but will help reduce stress because everyone knows the journey you're embarking on. Many people choose exercise or meditation as a way of destressing—give it a try. The other major thing that will bring you confidence you are taking the right next steps is if you live within your values. Treat other people well and display gratitude for the help you will no doubt receive along this journey.

5. *Start good habits and eliminate bad ones:* one of our most important ongoing goals should be personal development. If we are clear in our minds and our bodies and we feel great, we're more likely to achieve our goals. Start with something simple, such as removing yourself from your desk every few hours to take a 20-minute walk outside. During that walk I promise you that some of the issues you have been grappling with will be resolved in your mind. It also means eliminating some bad habits—which mostly means what you eat and drink, but can also be about how you treat others around you. Just remember, we all get stressed, but don't take it out on your most important support base.

6. *Don't get caught up in your expectations or the expectations of others:* when we were growing up, many of us wanted to be millionaires by the time we were 25 and then retire. Let's be realistic: we can't all achieve that. Set realistic goals and stick to them; don't chop and change depending on what other people say, unless you think they are being realistic. It's easy to see what other people have achieved and to want to be like them. You have your own skills and pathways, which can be just as powerful.

7. *Avoid negativity:* have a positive mindset. There will be failures in achieving goals and it's easy for others around you to remind you of those setbacks. At the same time, you can also be too hard on yourself. Accept that failure comes with success and embrace it. Always stay on the positive pathway.

8. *Work on your communication and management skills:* you probably can't achieve some of your goals without communicating them effectively to others—whether that's to raise funds, find clients or explain to your mentor

(continued)

what you're trying to achieve. Write down what your purpose is and practise your pitch to others, whether that be your friends or family. Confidence is the key to looking people in the eye so they see the determination of what you're trying to do. Your management skills are important. How you handle others in the office or even at home can have a big impact on achieving your goals. That doesn't mean you have to be aggressive to find your way, but you do need to have purpose.

9. *Learn something new every day:* we must always continue to read, research and ask questions of the people who can help us achieve our goals. It's surprising how a new piece of information can be a missing piece of the puzzle when it comes to decision making. Put some time aside every day for reading, whether it's in your lunch hour or just before you go to bed. In chapter 6 I listed the books that have had the most influence on my decision making.

10. *Think of how far you've come:* I know that reaching for your goals will be a marathon and not a sprint, and after a few months or even years it can be easy to feel like it's all too much. At that point, take a moment to reflect back on how far you've come and what you've achieved. It could be an investment fund that started with $500 and now has $5000 in it due to your savings and also smart investment decisions. Reward yourself when you need to with positive reflection.

Progress is about setting goals. The way you do that depends a great deal on your personal attitude and ability, so embrace opportunities.

Get away from all the noise and avoid things that can stop you achieving your goals.

There are many ways you can plan your week. Follow the QR code for the template I use to make sure I leverage almost every minute of my time. After I fill this out on Sunday night, I know my week is sorted and I can simply focus on the tasks that  need to be done and never waste a minute wondering, 'what should I do next?'. Download the template and learn to do more with less.

Clear the clutter

So now you've set your goals, created plans and consulted with the right experts, but there is still likely to be one major impediment lurking deep within you: self-inflected stress and the noise around you as everyone tries to give you advice.

Sometimes we still need to push some things aside to think and review clearly. Often meditation, which I practise daily, will help, but so can other forms of relaxation, such as exercise. Avoiding a range of things will help you achieve your goals. Here are a couple:

- *Dedicate your time and avoid distractions:* I know we're all addicted to our smartphones and the latest social media post or email, but various studies, including one published by George Mason University in the United States in August 2014, show that even the smallest distractions can have a significant impact on our understanding and productivity. It highlighted the impact of distractions on memory retention and multitasking: these two things are critical for obtaining the right research prior to investing. We know that information is king, so when you're planning and executing your goals, have a quiet, dedicated area if possible and take breaks to maximise your concentration. Many people prefer some music in the background, and that's fine, as long as it doesn't fall into the distraction category. This also means leaving your phone in another room or putting it on silent when you're using your laptop or PC.

- *Give yourself the best chance to excel:* we know we all work or plan better when we've had a good night's sleep or once we've eaten (preferably healthy food) and avoided such things as alcohol and drugs, which don't help with clear thinking. We also know that exercise gives our brain an endorphin hit, which the experts say helps reduce our stress and improves our outlook. Everyone has their own routine, but a morning when you're fresh from a good night's sleep, having done some exercise and before the emails or phone calls start to impact upon your day is a good morning, I'm sure you'll agree. This might be your sweet spot for planning and setting goals. Sometimes what I do is write down my plans for the next day just before I go to sleep and then review them again the next morning with a clear mind.

Clearly, the environment in which you operate can impact your concentration. Fortunately, this is addressable. If your concentration problems are more fundamental (including medical or psychological), then seek professional help. There are ways experts have highlighted to improve concentration—everything from becoming a crossword addict to taking up chess—but don't feel stressed if this whole process takes time and requires changes to your lifestyle or the elimination of old habits.

Planning and goal setting is important for helping you achieve the outcomes you are seeking, so take it seriously. Warn your family, like I do, that Sunday night before the working week is a time for reviewing and planning. That means when I disappear into my study everyone knows where I'm going and why. Shutting off both internal and external disturbances helps you to concentrate.

After you've set a daily or weekly activity list, be proud of it and refer to it as often as you wish. Take great joy in crossing off tasks as they are completed. Tackle the big jobs first because you know the smaller tasks will be easier to accomplish and won't feel as intimidating earlier in the day when you're likely to feel less tired.

Leverage yourself

It is important to try to be at the top of your game when making decisions. Understanding and adopting what I call 'field intelligence' (i.e. blocking out distractions—both visual and sound—when you're on the field of play) means being able to adjust quickly to the environment around you. Impediments could be competitive, government forced or just managing your employees. If you've ever heard a truly successful athlete or anyone at the top 1 per cent of their field talk, you'll know they have the ability to focus and block out noise and thoughts. Over time this becomes instinctive, and they develop field intelligence—that is, the ability to summon all their talent at the one time to perform.

Leveraging yourself is a big project in its own right. You will probably not be able to do it on your own. You need people and resources—and don't take for granted the resources you currently have at your disposal but haven't yet identified.

Think about everything you see around you every day: ideas that began with a thought once, long ago. Then consider not how to replicate these products or services, but how to leverage using these resources.

LET'S REFLECT ...

- Invest in your mental, physical, emotional and spiritual health. They are as important as your financial health.

- Embrace the 80/20 rule: set parameters for the things you can achieve most effectively and focus on them.

- Intelligent leverage begins with you. You must be motivated but there are many practices you can embrace that will help you significantly.

- Learn to do more with less. Set goals and establish techniques to meet those goals.

- Goal setting is empowering because it makes you feel like you're in control—but determine your own skills and pathways, and don't simply follow the expectations of others.

- Setbacks are inevitable, but stay on the positive pathway anyway because with failure comes success.

- Get away from the noise and all distractions: remain calm, focused and ready to execute.

- Remind yourself of the goals you need to set in order to leverage every aspect of your life with my 10 goals poster. Follow the QR code to download it, print it out, and post it in your office or workspace as a constant reminder of the long game journey you're on.

CHAPTER <u>9</u>

DECISION MAKING: ADOPT AN INVESTING MINDSET

My father used to recite a simple mantra: 'Prior Preparation Prevents Poor Performance'. We called it the five Ps. I now tell my teenage son the same thing, which must drive him mad.

When I started my career in law and funds management, I was young, but I had a deep-seated desire to achieve. That has never changed except now I work with some of the smartest investors in the world. They are like minded, and we work as a team to achieve great things. There is no ego among the most successful people because they are well established and have a proven track record. I'm fortunate to be associated with such people.

Preparation for me starts in front of the mirror early each morning where I might repeat to myself some of the key themes I'm going to share with my investors, colleagues or other people I have scheduled to meet that day.

That's also true for the end of the day as I compile all the necessary information I need for the following day—both in hard and soft copy—and have it nearby for when I wake up.

As I've already mentioned, I spend Sunday nights planning for the week ahead, including of course prioritising being with my family. They know not to bother me until well after dinner time on Sundays as I focus and visualise for the next week, and month, and set my goals in a clear and precise orderly format.

I focus on gratitude always. When you are prepared and have real gratitude for what you have in your life, it's impossible to also feel anger and fear.

Business strategist and multi-book author Tony Robbins highlights this in many of his speeches and books. I attended one of his events 30 years ago and his views have stayed with me: it's all about personal power. We need to recognise our true inner capabilities.

One of the key philosophies I try to pass on to the next generation is to always think about your old age when you're younger.

What influences investing decision making?

It's easy to think you've got the right investment strategy, and then, when you go to implement it, to find that it's not. Both external forces and internal ones can be powerful at derailing your plan.

When we make a decision to invest, we are constantly pushing against inbuilt bias, which is natural, and we need to be mindful of this.

These biases include:

- *Confirmation bias*

  We tend to seek out information that supports many of
  the views that we already hold. If we really love a stock
  on the share market or the thought of an investment
  property in a particular suburb, we will tend to go looking
  for information that might support that decision making.
  Equally, we might be so excited about purchasing a beach
  house for the lifestyle it offers that we won't go looking for
  information about why it doesn't make great investment
  sense. The more we read about or research whatever
  confirms our initial thoughts, the more determined we are
  to act upon that information. The way to stop this type of
  bias from influencing your decision making is to challenge
  the assumptions and take a fresh look at the investment
  case. It also pays to seeks a second opinion from your
  accountant or stockbroker—or if it's about real estate,
  someone who works in the industry but isn't involved in
  that transaction. It's important to stop, revisit and rethink
  before acting

- *Information bias*

  We are bombarded with information all the time.
  Sometimes it comes from an email or social media and
  sometimes it's when we take a look at news sites or receive
  related reports from stockbrokers or real estate agents.
  Everyone might be talking up a particular investment
  opportunity if they're selling. Equally, if the media turns
  on a company or a CEO all potential investors will hear
  or read about is negative news, which might turn them
  off. The critical thing is to go back over the fundamentals

of a potential investment opportunity and avoid the noise around it. Remember, most investments should be considered as a longer term holding for when whatever is newsworthy right now is likely to have passed. Remember also, when there is significant negative commentary around a particular stock its share price might be temporarily below fair value and offer good upside. However, you should generally ignore day-to-day share movements and only ever act on the best available research

- *Downside bias*

  All investors worry about an investment doing poorly and making a loss and this concern tends to overpower any decision making. It's a natural bias since we all work hard for our money and don't want to lose it. This bias is not only influential when it comes to an investor procrastinating or delaying an investment decision, but also when putting off selling a stock that might be falling in value, hoping that it will rebound and they won't end up losing money. The reality is that a badly performing stock might just keep declining or at worst a company can fall into bankruptcy. Often, retirees in particular fall into their downside bias because they are worried about the nest egg they will pass on to the next generation and would prefer to be more secure in their investment decision making. This, of course, is particularly understandable

- *Incentive-driven bias*

  We are all aware of the selling techniques of sales people, from real estate agents to accountants, pushing investment products. In Australia's financial system there is a chain of financial incentives to encourage people to buy various products. Mortgage brokers get a commission if people switch loans; financial planners sometimes receive incentives if people buy a product from them — an incentive that, by the way, should be declared. A stockbroking firm typically receives a fee of between 1 and 2 per cent of the total transaction they handle. Australia had a banking Royal Commission in 2017 based on the lack of transparency provided to customers around the services being offered. Watch out for the tell-tale signs of hard sell or short time frames. There are also incentive schemes within companies to generate higher and higher profits, sometimes for the short term rather than the long term. My preference is for companies with internal systems that incentivise management on both the downside (thus protecting shareholder returns) and the upside, with mechanisms that make it in their best interests to return any excess funds to shareholders. An example of this could be share-option programs that excessively lean toward executive compensation instead of reinvestment, which could lead to management behaviour that may not suit a shareholder's long-term interests.

- *Hindsight bias*

There is a tenancy to look back with rose-coloured glasses and become too optimistic about the future by dismissing past failures in an investment as the fault of the market or the CEO (who has since moved on), or suggesting external factors such as interest rate movements might have played a role. Of course, this might just ignore the fundamentals of a bad investment and why you shouldn't repeat that same mistake. We are only human and we like to block out our mistakes, but you should maintain independent, rational thinking when it comes to investment decision making and embrace past mistakes to be avoided—don't ignore them

- *Keep-it-simple bias*

  Making the right investment decisions can be complex. We are bombarded with so much information that we often just want to believe the simplest explanation for why we should or shouldn't go ahead with an investment. It might be the media rockstar CEO or the management team we've followed for years and won't hear a bad thing about. Or it might be the location of an investment property we're fixated on, without considering alternatives that might be cheaper and offer better rental yields. To overcome this bias, write down a detailed investment case for each form of investment you'd like to consider and go beyond the simplest explanation

- *Bandwagon bias*

  We never like to miss out on a great investment opportunity or feel that the rest of the world has jumped onboard one without us. But as we all know, falling into the trap of 'group think' is dangerous. This is my warning against people 'following the follower'. An example of this is the Buy Now Pay Later stock bubble of 2019 to 2021 in Australia, which later burst when the market worked out it was just another form of lay-by. These companies were, and remain, grossly overvalued and should be avoided. The multiple on these companies should be trading around 8 to 12 times net profit—not 50 times. Dumb!

While you shouldn't seek to be a contrarian for the sake of being a contrarian, have no hesitation in taking, as Robert Frost said, 'the road less travelled', if that's what your analysis concludes

- *Greed bias*

  We are all tempted by money and the benefits that it brings. Sometimes, if we have a win on an investment, such as a win at the races, we want more of it. But there are no sure winners, so a stock that has enjoyed significant capital gains might not keep rising if you buy significantly more shares. Sometimes you also have to know when to sell. All investors feel they can show restraint, except when they're in the middle of a boom, hoping to milk it for all they can before the bust. That's why the smartest investors talk constantly about having a balanced fund, so winners can be offset by losers and in time the total value of the portfolio keeps rising

- *Probability bias*

  Every decision we make is based on the probability of outcomes. When it comes to investment, it's the same. We do our research, we build a business case for the investment and we include the possible positive and negative influences. How we balance up those probabilities often comes down to our own inherent optimistic or pessimistic outlook. That means some people overestimate the challenges and decline the opportunity to invest and others embrace the best possible outlook. There are ways of better understanding where the probability bias falls, such as the difference between a well-known blue-chip stock with an earnings track record and a speculative stock that has yet to earn a profit but shows strong future prospects. We know that the speculative stock carries more risk, but also possibly more return. Sometimes an investor can balance out the probabilities. For example, investing in both traditional utilities — which offer reliable performance because we all depend on energy (but which still rely largely on fossil fuels, meaning investors will need to fundamentally change their business model over time) — and investing in emerging solar technologies, which are likely to grow in significance. Another error investors make is to overestimate or misprice the risk of low-probability events. Travel stocks in Australia collapsed after COVID-19 because of lockdowns and international travel restrictions yet have recovered quickly since the travel boom took hold in 2022. Now people can't get enough of international travel as they revenge spend. Generally, the risk of a permanent capital loss from a 'black swan' event in a broader portfolio can be low.

Again don't be influenced by what's hip right now, or by what Warren Buffet calls 'today's headlines' in newspapers because they will soon become recycling paper at best.

- *Anchoring bias*

We all start our investment decision making from a particular anchor. If it's share investing, that's mostly the current share price or perhaps the recent trend — upwards or downwards. Some even take it further by charting a company's share price for years. Unfortunately, past share movements cannot predict the future and that's where an investor has to focus on the company fundamentals.

The same is true if you're looking for an investment property. House prices might have jumped in a particular area, which attracts the attention of investors. The question is whether prices are now overvalued or still have an upside. Investors also need to consider rental yields and the annual return on their investment and not just the value of the property.

Knowledge vs fear

It all comes down to the old battle between knowledge and fear. When knowledge is high or present, fear drops, and the reverse is true when fear raises its head.

LEVERAGE: GUIDING THE NEXT GENERATION

To improve our knowledge base and counter negative outcomes, I am quite frequently asked what topics or areas of study we should be steering our next generation of children towards, including instilling in them the importance of leverage.

My response on every occasion is that our younger generation should be embracing several real-life priorities, including:

- *Mathematics:* having a good understanding of numbers and some accounting skills is critical. Numbers are my life—I use them during most of my working hours.

- *Speech:* public speaking is a great skill, but even in normal conversations, be sure to have something to contribute and don't waste anyone's time. I don't believe

(continued)

people really pause and think before they speak. Think again, and slowly explain your position. If you don't have something productive and complementary to say, don't worry about speaking at all.

- *Presentation:* I know things are a lot more casual in the post-COVID-19 era, but I still think the first time you meet a person, you assess their appearance. Whether that's their dress, their suit, their shirt, their tie or their shoes, I think it's important. The second test is the next 90 seconds and what comes out of their mouth. You can discover, if you listen closely enough, the level of intelligence, experience, passion and energy a person can display in the first 90 seconds of a conversation.

- *Networking:* having the talent to network is by far the most powerful skill you can possess and teach someone. The ability to earn trust and be given the time to be heard by those you admire in your workplace, your industry or in the community is a powerful thing. Remember it's about listening, and great networks can have a tremendous impact on your life and your family both now and for generations to come.

Author Adam Smith, in his book *The bravest you: 5 steps to fight your biggest fears, find your passion and unlock your extraordinary life,* ranks the 10 top roadblocks to success as:

1. *Fear of inadequacy*: not being skilled enough

2. *Fear of uncertainty*: being afraid of the unknown

3. *Fear of failure*: worrying that something will go wrong

4. *Fear of rejection*: being concerned that failure will inevitably come

5. *Fear of missing out*: always wanting what someone else has

6. *Fear of change*: not being content with life's shifts

7. *Fear of losing control*: accepting that change means losing some control, but it should be in moderation

8. *Fear of being judged*: facing the judgement of others—from our boss to our friends

9. *Fear of something bad happening*: worrying about fear that's outside a person's control

10. *Fear of getting hurt*: accepting that life happens, but we must embrace it.

These fears must be identified early in your life and overcome. The only way that can happen is with practice, drill and rehearsal (PDR). The mantra of 'I can do this, and it will be done' was, and is still, one of my favourites.

LET'S REFLECT ...

- Focus on gratitude because it's impossible to feel anger and fear simultaneously with gratitude. It's about having personal power and recognising your true inner capabilities.

- Whenever you make an investment decision there's an inbuilt bias that will influence your decision making. That's normal, but it's good to be aware of the various biases people tend to have.

- To beat your biases, it's important to stop, revisit and rethink before acting. Go back over the fundamentals of a potential investment opportunity and avoid the noise around it.

- The smartest investors have balanced funds so that winners can be offset by losers and the total value of the portfolio keeps rising.

- Don't look back at past share price movements. Instead, try to look forward at prospects. Don't follow the follower.

- Think about the distribution curve: the future might not produce the most optimal outcome for a stock or investment, but equally, sometimes markets overestimate the downward trend.

- Fill yourself with knowledge: it will help reduce your fear levels.

CHAPTER <u>10</u>

RISK MITIGATION: HOW TO LEVERAGE INSURANCE AND HEDGING

One of the keys to investment success is to reduce risks. We always look at the upside, but there will inevitably be a downside.

Hamilton-Chase Pty Ltd, the company I started, is a funds management business that manages more than $21 billion, sourced from large international institutions to family offices and high-net-worth individuals.

That's a big exposure to the market, so of course we do everything in our power to reduce risk. Some of that comes in the form of asset allocation; some of it increasingly will come from the use of technology such as AI to predict future trends. Ultimately, there are some tried and tested tools that can help mitigate risk.

The bottom line is trends can change quickly and you will need protection when it comes to an investment strategy. Just look at why insurance companies have the power they possess today and can dramatically influence the present and future via their underwriting influence in business globally—probably much more than they did pre-COVID-19, given their painful experience during the pandemic. The key here is to anticipate change.

There are two types of traditional risk management policy: insurance and hedging.

Insure to cover your assets

Insurance has always been entwined with finance. As far back as 4000 BCE, when merchants transported goods by sea they would take out contracts to protect themselves. These 'bottomry contracts' shielded merchants from having to repay the loans that they took out to finance voyages if the goods were lost at sea. In fact, it was the maritime industry globally that led the way for developing insurance, which recognises the growing importance of trade and commerce and the natural human inclination to worry and plan if things take a turn for the worse.

Natural disasters were a driving force for evoking change. The greatest of these, when it came to the insurance industry, was the Great Fire of London in 1666. For the first time, people could obtain building insurance cover for fire. The rise of commerce in the growing British Empire also saw established insurance companies move away from the previous speculative companies' practice of trying to sign up customers without paying out claims. Three companies in Britain were the driving forces behind property and later liability insurance: the London Assurance Corporation, the Royal Exchange Assurance company and then—in 1688—Lloyd's of London, which began as a coffee house.

The next time someone underestimates the importance of coffee to bring people together and conduct business (how many coffee meetings do you have a week?), remind them of Lloyd's of London. This is where bankers and underwriters could come together in the one place to negotiate and exchange insurance contracts. And back then, the 'underwriter', or person providing the risk funds, would actually put their name under the contract — if only we had such accountability today.

What made the role of underwriters easier and insurance cheaper for the masses was the mathematical prowess of famous Frenchman Blaise Pascal, in 1654, whose probability theory influenced insurance risk management strategies. If underwriters better understood the risk, they could better price the policy.

It wasn't long before the Americans caught on to the importance of insurance. Great minds such as Benjamin Franklin helped to found the first American insurance company (formed to insure buildings from fire damage), called the Philadelphia Contributionship, in 1752. They were ahead of their time because they knew a few things about marketing: their slogan was 'Hand in Hand' and they created a 'fire mark' logo that illustrated this sentiment. The logo was posted on a square board attached to the wall of any property that had fire insurance covered by the company. Back then Philadelphia Contributionship didn't need social media to illustrate its coverage in the local community. Remarkably, the company still exists today.

It's not surprising that since that time the world's biggest insurance companies have been primarily based in the United States or Europe — and they follow the path to the growth in trade and finance.

New products started to emerge: life insurance (once mortality rates were better understood) followed by the reinsurance industry, which evolved to offer third-party investors a return if they also took on part of the portfolio of risk. Reinsurance has helped save many insurance companies when a big disaster event occurs and they face massive payouts.

What does this history lesson mean today? Throughout the ages, people have always found a way to spread their risk, and today insurance is a sophisticated leveraging tool that should always be considered as part of any investment strategy.

On a personal level, we should all have life insurance and, if you run a business, income protection insurance. Of course, that depends on your financial resources and the current debt position. Running a business involves taking out business insurance to protect against claims of negligence and to safeguard the business's assets. Then there's professional indemnity insurance, and these days cyber-attack insurance policies are also important. The key is to do your homework and find the right policy to fit your circumstances.

But when it comes to investing, sadly there is no traditional insurance policy you can take out if your stock or security falls significantly in value — except, of course, hedging.

Hedge to minimise risk

Most hedging is used in derivative products such as put options or futures, which we've already learned about in this book. That's where an investor will make an investment based on the value of stock or some form of asset moving in a particular direction in the future — either up or down. But human nature means we are worrying what happens if it moves in exactly the opposite direction. Well that's called taking a hedge position and investors can buy another derivative to protect themselves from it.

A wide range of options and futures contracts offer investors the ability to safeguard their investments against unfavourable price fluctuations across a diverse array of assets such as bonds, stocks, interest rates and commodities, currencies.

Of course there is always what investors like to call a risk–reward trade-off when it comes to hedging. If you're an investor and you believe a security is going to move in a particular way (and it does), by taking out a hedge you'll reduce your return on your investment. Most investors don't take out a perfect 100 per cent hedge because that would be around the same cost as taking out the original derivative, so sometimes they just partially cover themselves and they only do it for a limited period of time, because the longer the hedge is open the more the cost. Overall the price of the hedge depends on the risks associated with the adverse outcome you are protecting yourself from.

For most investors, the best hedge doesn't involve buying the more sophisticated derivative products (leave that up to the big corporates involved in global trade and the professional investors) but diversifying your investment portfolio. This is called a natural hedge.

You can hedge in many ways, using different asset classes (from risky, such as tech start-ups, to less risky, such as cash investments), different forms of investment (shares vs property) or hedging within a particular asset class (creating an asset-neutral share portfolio (blue chips vs small cap—that is, well-researched—stocks).

Spread hedging is slightly different because it involves taking two different derivative positions on the same asset (offering a spread on potential outcomes, which might fall somewhere in the middle) and is often used to manage changes to indexes. What that means is an investor might buy two put options: one with a high strike price and another with a lower strike price. That means no matter how the stock moves you can be covered. Of course it also means you limit your returns.

HEDGING WITH A PUT OPTION

Put options sound complicated but they can be navigated, particularly when it comes to implementing a hedge.

Let's just remind ourselves of what a put option is: it is a contract for a specific period of time giving the owner the right to sell a security at a pre-set price. How does this work as a hedge? Well you might have bought shares expecting them to rise, but if for some unexpected reason they drop sharply, then they will be sold before the price falls too far at the price you've set, meaning you have limited your losses.

For example, if you buy 1000 shares of a stock at $10 per share (total outlay $10 000), you could then buy a put option with a strike price of $8 (that would expire in one year) to hedge your investment. With this put, you could then sell for $8 your 1000 shares any time in the next year.

How does that compare to your initial investment? Well, that depends on the price of the put option, but generally they are much less than the price of the security. For this example, let's assume the put option is $1 per share or $1000 in total. If the stock is trading at $12 one year later, you will not exercise the option and will be out of pocket $1000 for the cost of the option. That's okay, though, because your unrealised gain on the investment so far is $2000 so you're still $1000 ahead, with the hope of the share price continuing to rise. You've also had the comfort of knowing for 12 months you've been covered against serious losses.

On the other hand, let's assume the stock does fall to $8 within the one year of the contract and that triggers the required sale of the shares (before they fall further). That means you're out of pocket $2000 on your investment, plus the cost of the option, which you'll remember was $1000 ($3000 in total). Now let's assume that the shares fall to becoming worthless. If the put option hadn't triggered your entire share sale, your losses would have been $10 000 compared to $3000 with the hedge—leaving you with $7000 in your pocket.

The pros and cons of hedging

As I alluded to earlier in the book, money is like soap: the more you play with it, the less you have! And so it is with hedging.

Among the pros of hedging are:

- The higher up the highwire (risk curve) we are as investors, the more we like to have a safety net underneath.

- The cost of a derivative hedge is usually a fraction of the cost of the security you are looking to protect.

- Hedging might look complicated but there are easier ways of doing it, such as diversifying your portfolio.

The cons of hedging include:

- There is an additional cost to buying a derivative hedge on top of the cost of actually buying the security attached to the trade.

- There is no guarantee you'll ever use the hedge — it depends on the strike price and the movement in the value of the security or asset being protected.

- There is no guarantee a hedge will completely mitigate your losses.

- It is difficult to precisely assess the risk of a hedge and whether it is value for money.

For many investors, hedging, or a derivative contract, will never come into play in their day-to-day financial activities or trading plans. Instead, many investors have a long-term strategy in mind, meaning that any short-term fluctuations are ignored as it's likely their investment will grow with the market. Of course, it's still important to observe trends over time, and whether investment portfolios need to be adjusted. Unlike some other large investors, I'm always prepared to sit and hold when I'm unsure. When you feel comfortable you've got the investment mix about right.

For long-term investors there may not be a need to learn about hedging. Remember, investors may indirectly hedge because the large companies in which they invest or the investment funds they are a member of (such as large super funds) tend to engage in hedging practices on a regular basis — particularly on things such as currencies (if they invest overseas) or commodities (if, for example, they are a resource company with forward contracts). In this way the investor is indirectly protected as a shareholder.

Nevertheless, if you want to understand how the big players operate, it can be useful to understand how hedging works.

LET'S REFLECT ...

- Options and futures contracts enable investors to safeguard their investments against unfavourable price fluctuations across a diverse array of assets.

- Trends can change quickly and you will need protection when it comes to an investment strategy.

- Insurance is a concept that has allowed commerce to grow strongly for centuries. It must form an important basis for any investor protecting their assets.

- Hedging is an essential financial risk-minimising tool that is in frequent use in financial markets. It allows investors to take an opposite position in the market from the primary form of investment. That means if the price of the security moves contrary to investor expectation, potential losses can be mitigated.

- Derivatives such as a future, forward or options contract are the most common forms of hedging.

- The most effective hedge is often just ensuring you have a diversified investment portfolio.

CHAPTER 11

ARTIFICIAL INTELLIGENCE: THE NEXT LEVERAGING TOOL

Technology changes our lives every day. The reality is that it's preferable to obtain quality data and information via technology as we can more effectively share information in real time. Remember when everyone used to buy the newspaper to check yesterday's stock prices? I say stop relying on yesterday's race guide. Yesterday's stock pages in the newspapers show what's happened in the rear vision mirror.

It's been widely reported that at the beginning of the 20th century information was doubling every 500 years, yet by 2018 it was doubling every 18 months.

The next generation is artificial intelligence (AI), which has captured the imagination of the market in recent times. We know AI is being enhanced by the tech giants all the time. I'd say the information age is moving today at 500 per cent of where we were in 2018.

Smart investors have always established parameters and built in their own investment system run by a step-by-step process that, importantly, monitors progress in real time. Now the future will be more predictive.

Technology and algorithms

What has certainly come about in the past 10 years is the power of algorithms in relation to technology. One of the most fascinating breakthroughs with technology, thanks to companies such as Google and Microsoft and for that matter Elon Musk, is that computers can operate without human intervention based on algorithm trend movements.

In investing terms this means they can anticipate volatility, which enables the user to mitigate and manage risk. I have found it very, very helpful in decision making in my own company when spreading investments.

In fact at Hamilton-Chase Pty Ltd we developed our own AI technology, at a cost of $25 million. It can stress test portfolios against likely market movements and add in a range of influencing factors, including geo-political potential shifts, climate forecasts and their dangers, expected federal and state taxation shifts. It is able to scan back through more than 50 years of data to consider likely moves in more than 22000 different asset instruments. I like to call it my 'black box'—which the technology experts who helped create it hate. Its actual name is 'Conquer'™, for obvious reasons, and it's used exclusively by my team for assisted guidance for our private clientele.

The expert systems and data mining are gathered in over 200 fields and increase every year. Their objective is to mitigate risk and to seek higher-than-average returns with less-than-average risk. The decisions I have made over my 35-year investment career have—in particular over the past few years—been particularly accurate due to the data producing information and signalling my own blind spots. After making this calculation, I worked out that this process with human intervention and data systems mining has saved me $200 000 000 in financial carnage.

What comes out are predictions about which assets are most likely to be impacted by interest rate rises and falls, bond rate rises and falls or the likely volatility in companies that are listed or, for that matter, not listed. The measures that can be imputed into a computer aim to mitigate losses, including in the areas that we were never able to include in analyses, such as likely probability of floods, bushfires, storms, tornados and earthquakes.

AI can assist with identifying undervalued stocks and commodities, and which areas of the property market are likely to either outperform or underperform when evaluating or making investment decisions. Of course, it all comes down to the skill of the code writers, which is paramount in forecasting and making decisions both for investments and for overall business development. We shouldn't fear technology as it's a great counterbalance to the increasingly challenging world we live in today. Algorithms, or data mining and expert systems, are critical for developing such technology.

The skill of forecasting

Most fund managers and investment experts continue to make decisions based on little or poor probability heavily weighted to yesterday's or last year's performance (or 'yesterday's race guide').

However, this mostly proven past historical data will have little or no bearing on what we should do or prepare for in the next 12 months, 3 years, 5 years, 10 years and beyond.

I have been quoted in Australian newspaper articles and other media outlets giving a forecast and view on what I thought of the coming 12 to 18 months in a certain market, or how events would play out over time, particularly in the areas of property trends, macro economies and overall business environment changes that were about to occur. These forecasts have been very accurate. This was based initially on my view and feel of the market at the time but had to be measured or verified by data and not human assessments.

To successfully or productively predict the market and/or be accurate (that is, by 85 per cent + or more) requires over 200 fields and/or ratios, probabilities — some mathematical, statistical and behavioural or reactionary. I don't believe computers alone can predict the market shifts that will occur with great accuracy just yet. But I will say this: computers may just be able to influence the market and persuade people around how to think, which can then become the reality for them.

Of course, too much dependency on forecasting with expert systems, data mining and mimicking without a good understanding and experience of the field at this point would be, in my opinion, reckless and irresponsible. To be a great investor or businessperson, dashboard assistance is all it should be at present, helping to navigate through the intellectual game of business and investing.

Great investors such as Warren Buffet don't rely on technology. Buffet carefully studies any business he considers investing in and talks to its people. He probably also doesn't look at a computer daily. It is said that he doesn't carry a mobile phone and doesn't have time for Teams or Zoom meetings.

What's striking about Buffet, and I was lucky enough to shake his hand once at a Berkshire meeting, is his natural processing ability to base his decision making on a set of guiding financial metrics covered in this book, based on what makes sense to him, what works now and what will be successful in the future.

Buffet's best skill and talent is that he reads and reads — everything from daily financial newspapers (he now owns many newspapers) to many other financial reports every day — like a forensic scientist.

I like to keep my head clear and grounded in business and rely on data to support my theory. Interestingly, the Conquer™ technology has been more useful in predicting assets to avoid than those to acquire. This leads to reverse financial engineering. Determining what not to invest in leaves working out what's left and where the market capital will flow to over the short, medium and long term.

AI technology as leverage

As AI technology continues to improve, no doubt for the next generation of investors, it will become an even greater leverage. It becomes particularly important for avoiding losses or taking a defensive approach to investing, which is what I like about it: playing for the long term.

Vary rarely do you see an offensive strategy work well consistently. Defensive players in business, sport and life do better over the long term.

You only need to look at Ray Dalio, scholar and best-selling author of the book *Principles,* to see why we need to focus more on the 'downside' of risk. Dalio founded Bridgewater, the world's biggest hedge fund. He's the grandfather of what he called 'risk parity', or having a balanced portfolio. Dalio believed in a mix of 'four seasons' investments: those offering higher returns than inflation, those expecting a lower return on inflation, those expecting a higher return than economic growth and those (at least in the short-term) expecting returns lower than economic growth (but offering far less risk). He would pour scorn on funds that had 90 per cent of their funds in equities and overexposed themselves to risk.

I have spent most of my investing life focusing on the downside and building a defensive strategy. The classic examples of just focusing on the upside—such as the Buy Now Pay Later bubble, cryptocurrencies and digital currencies that flourished in the unregulated boom of 2019 to 2021 (when almost none of the companies were making any profits)—was that investors focused on future earnings. This was a classic example of investing in 'hope' (there's that term again).

As a rule, if the company doesn't turn a profit in year one, I'm not your guy! I've seen too many people throw money at audacious, poorly managed product and service companies only to be greatly disappointed.

The good news is algorithms and technology don't tend to run with the pack if programmed for a final determination. It can be useful, for example, to look for trends as our population, shifts in demographics and we, for example, focus and spend more on healthcare. In the future, the companies I'm looking at are those investing in genetic molecular research, population DNA analysis and the genetic likelihood of future health events in individuals. Interestingly, while they have enormous upside, they can easily fit into a defence strategy as well. My aim, with the use of technology, is to always carve out a portfolio of assets that is close to 70 per cent defence and 30 per cent offence.

***

So, if you think that all this technology and AI probability and predictability is a mere whim and not worth a closer look, then study it and think again. In most Western economies, governments and institutions have been using collective data derived from you via every piece of official paper you've ever filled in for their own formulated policy design systems for almost 90 years. This will only accelerate in the future digital era.

For example, tax file numbers were introduced to forecast and monitor country revenues, but today they tell us so much more about tax avoidance trends and many other things. The ATAR (Australian Tertiary Admission Rank) or SAT (Scholastic Aptitude Test, as it is called in the United States) gathers information to determine trends in academic study and whether students are developing the skills for the required jobs and industries of the future.

On the downside, poor educational data or declining socio-economic trends can help determine the likelihood of increased crime rates or poor societal engagement, which may lead to increased jail populations, something that governments will need to plan for.

LET'S REFLECT ...

- The next generation of investment risk managers is likely to be driven by AI technology and algorithms as the tech giants are constantly enhancing AI.

- Computers can operate without human intervention based on algorithm trend movements.

- In investing terms, the power of algorithms in AI technology means they can anticipate volatility, enabling the user to mitigate and manage risk.

- AI will be able to help identify possible future volatility as well as under-performing asset classes or stocks.

- As a form of leverage, AI technology is particularly important for avoiding losses or taking a defensive approach to investing.

- AI doesn't run with the pack and isn't influenced by emotion. It's likely in the near future to be available not just to institutional investors, but to the masses.

PART II: KEY TAKEAWAYS

- Intelligent leverage is a multi-faceted process that involves you focusing on your time, money and networking opportunities. The tools are available, but you must take control of them. This requires daily focused thought.

- Start your empowerment process by leveraging yourself: look at how you manage everything from your health and your sleep to investing in building your knowledge and network base.

- Accept that every investment decision you make will be influenced by some form of bias.

- Hedging and obtaining the right asset insurance are important for advanced risk management.

- Artificial intelligence is the next leveraging tool—control it, but don't be afraid of it.

PART III

HONING THE SKILL OF INTELLIGENT LEVERAGE

CHAPTER 12

ACHIEVEMENT: KNOW WHAT YOU WANT

Famed American author Napoleon Hill (who wrote one of my favourite books, *Think and Grow Rich*) argued with successful American businessman and philanthropist Clement W Stone for decades on what was the number-one principle of the law of success.

The debate was about whether a 'positive mental attitude' or a 'definiteness of purpose' was more important.

For Hill it was definiteness of purpose and for Stone it was about having a positive mental attitude.

Sadly, neither of these men is alive today for me to ask (Clement W Stone amazingly lived to 100 and died in 2002), but I believe 'definiteness of purpose' sits just ahead 'positive mental attitude'.

The main reason that the most successful people I have read about—some of whom I've been fortunate to meet in person—achieved what they did is that what made them successful was an obvious standout trait that they possessed ahead of all others: a terrific sense of empowerment, confidence and fearlessness. They had a great understanding of what they were pursuing and developed the necessary skills to obtain and succeed in that pursuit.

It's evident that it is crucial to develop a clear, well-engineered plan; this is superior to having a positive mental attitude, which some people are just naturally blessed to have in abundance. Creating a plan requires deep thought and then execution. Of course, I'm not saying a positive mental attitude isn't important, as it comes a close second, but first you must crack the code or develop the formula for what you're seeking to achieve.

More often, they go hand in hand (no wonder Hill and Stone argued and frequently debated) because to develop the plan requires clear thinking.

It's easy for me to say, I know, but I recommend, where possible, surrounding yourself with people who not only support you, but also challenge you to do better (including mentoring you). This relationship should be a two-way street and you should always feel a sense of gratitude for those around you, especially your family, as they all play a huge part in your mental capacity to keep moving forward.

KNOW WHAT YOU WANT TO ACHIEVE

Here are my top five building blocks for working towards what you're trying to achieve.

1. *Know your purpose*

   The starting point of all achievement is being clear in what you'd like to achieve. Life can quickly pass you by without a plan for doing something with it. Sometimes that means bouncing ideas or having a mentor to provide feedback. Remember, there are many others who have successfully grown a business or who have specific investment strategies and who would be powerful allies. This was dubbed 'The Mastermind Principle' by Napoleon Hill, who described it as an alliance of two or more minds working in perfect harmony for the attainment of a common definite objective. Sometimes success does not come without the co-operation of others.

You also must believe in and back yourself. That means putting time and energy as well as finances behind your idea. Some people call this applying faith to your idea or plan. It can also mean going the extra mile, having that extra meeting, staying up a little later to workshop your ideas on a Zoom call or reading that research document on a company you'd like to back by investing in it. The so-called spiritual 'law of compensation'—that is, the relationship between effort and reward—often comes into play.

2. *Have the right attitude*

A positive mental attitude has probably got you to where you are right now, which is thinking about how to improve your future and unlocking the tools for intelligent leverage. Success often attracts more success. The more confident you are in meetings, searching out the right mentors or proposing your idea to financiers, the more likely you are to impress the people you are making a connection with. Unleash your personality, which is a sum of your mental, spiritual and physical traits. Often your attitude will distinguish you from others. It's one important factor

(continued)

149

that helps determine the opinion others have of you or the idea that you are pitching. Remember, when it comes to creating an investment strategy sometimes it means going outside your comfort zone: attending a conference seminar, joining the discussion in a relevant blog or being prepared to reach out to a company with a series of questions if you're looking to invest in them.

3. *Maintain your self-discipline*

Self-discipline can mean many things. It means sticking to your idea and backing it in the face of initial criticism. It can also mean budgeting to save the funds you need to create an investment fund or paying for the right financial advice, which requires other lifestyle sacrifices. Self-discipline also calls for balancing your emotions and reasoning with what your head is telling you, which means knowing when to pull out if you think an idea or investment may be the wrong one.

Self-discipline generates what is sometimes called 'controlled attention', or the ability to completely focus on your object and put the actions required into place.

4. *Embrace adversity and defeat*

There will be failures—for example, investments that don't work out or a plan for business growth that doesn't find a market. Experience will ensure the next move you make is even better. Remember that failures should be viewed as temporary defeats and sometimes they are blessings in disguise.

During these difficult times, find a release for your stress: go for a run or embrace other forms of exercise. Take a break from your project and speak to those you can trust. Every successful leader had some setback or failure.

5. *Develop the right habits*

While reading this book you're hopefully taking note of all the things you need to do to leverage yourself. Look after your health, meditate if that helps and invest in the people who support you, such as your family. It's amazing that if you start doing this you'll fall into the right habits and look back in six months and realise you've transformed your life. These habits will allow you to face your challenges and help you plan for the next phase of your financial transformation.

Stay positive

Sometimes it's good to put well-known positive quotes on your desk or pin them to your computer to remind you to keep focused. Further down, I'll list some well-known positive quotes I often refer to. Most of them come from a very famous radio announcer in the United States called Earl Nightingale. Earl wasn't a household name in Australia, but he was in the United States. His broadcasts were taken by over 1000 radio stations and ran for decades. In the United States he got the nickname 'Dean of Personal Development'. Today it is possible to still get audiobooks of some of his best work. If you have the chance, put one on in the car. He's one of the most listened to people in American history and lived his life true to what he told people. Earl died in 1989 at the age of 68. Here are some of his best pearls of wisdom.

- 'Learn to enjoy every minute of your life.'

  To me this means embracing gratitude and thinking about what you have in your life right now and why you are already successful in so many ways. As I've said before, when you think of and feel gratitude, fear and anger slowly dissipate.

- 'Don't let the fear of the time it will take to accomplish something stand in the way of doing it.

  There have been many projects in my life that have taken considerable time to come to fruition. Sometimes I put them on the backburner and then return to them later. Time is always relative.

- 'Whatever we plant in our subconscious mind and nourish with repetition and emotion will one day become a reality.'

  I find it powerful to visualise in my mind what I'm trying to achieve. I often do this while I'm meditating. I can see what I want to achieve and that's a big motivating force.

- Think about the progress you've already made—Nightingale called this your 'acres of diamonds'—whether that's getting your first investment property or even just putting aside $1000 for your first investment fund. This can also mean being grateful for the family who surround you. Remember, you're on the pathway to greater financial independence and although it can sometimes get hard, it will be worth it.

Nightingale also maintained that getting rich should never be your objective. Aspire and create; then the rewards will follow—not just financially but in your relationships and wellbeing as well.

Another one of my favourite quotes is by existential psychologist and author Rollo May: 'The opposite of courage in our society is not cowardice, it is conformity'. In other words, don't follow the follower. Plan your own pathway to financial strength. Do your research and seek out the best outcomes for you and your family. This is especially important when it comes to retirement planning.

So what does all this mean?

You're not alone. You can find inspiration in the journey others have taken, the challenges they have met and how they have trained their minds to keep moving forward. When it gets hard, go back and read these inspirational quotes to ease and eliminate your stress.

LET'S REFLECT ...

- Having a purpose and a positive mental attitude go hand in hand; you can't have one without the other.
- The standout trait of high achievers is a terrific sense of empowerment, confidence and fearlessness.
- Know your purpose, have a positive attitude, maintain self-discipline, embrace adversity and defeat, and develop good habits: these are the building blocks for knowing what you want to achieve.
- Staying on track means seeking out those who will help you and support and mentor your idea. Embrace their contribution, but also be grateful for their help.
- Appreciate what you already have and visualise what you'd like to achieve. Visualisation is a powerful motivator.
- There will always be challenges in life, but there are also ways to stay positive and keep a clear mind.

CHAPTER 13

PLANNING: THE KEY TO INTELLIGENT LEVERAGE

As you read earlier, I can't stress enough the importance of planning if you want to leverage your life and finances intelligently — so remember these three words: *plan, plan, plan.*

There's no magic recipe for success. Planning is essential for your personal life and your financial life. You should plan on a weekly, monthly and yearly basis. As you know, I make a point of setting 20 goals annually.

Set ongoing milestones

Here's a list of things you should consider at each interval of your planning routine:

- *Weekly*
  - List the must-do and major goals that enhance your life.

— Make calls and seek the assistance of others to grow and enhance your ideas.

— Maintain the housekeeping items (including the paperwork) that are necessary to keep your goals and family intact.

- *Monthly*

  — Set targets that are realistic and critical to achieving one-twelfth of your yearly goals.

  — Instigate the changes to habits that are needed for the yearly results to materialise.

  — Organise a check-in with your investment planner/ accountant or business partners, customers and of course family to ensure you are at peace and in harmony with your goals.

- *Yearly*

  — Undertake a rigorous check that your yearly goals are on track (or hopefully achieved) and don't fall behind on sticking to your calendar of events and milestones.

  — Spend some quality time reflecting on what has been achieved so far for the year.

  — Set your yearly goals for the next year (some of them might spill over from last year—that's okay; don't be too hard on yourself) but remember: *do not* let time or anyone prevent you from achieving them.

When we plan, we are strongly guided by our goals—whether they are to increase our income, reduce our debt, put money aside for a particular investment or save for a holiday we've been putting off for years.

Let's start with financial goals (which includes investment planning). The right planning impacts our behaviour: how much you save and spend, and ensuring you have enough liquidity available in case of an emergency or an unexpected event.

Have annual strategies

Here are 10 financial planning strategies you should consider at least once a year:

1. *Review your life and health insurance.* Do you have the right cover? Have your circumstances changed? Are you paying too much for your cover? These are just some of the questions you should consider.

2. *Review your income and expenditure.* Are you living beyond your means? Has your income changed and if so, why? Do you have a spending budget for the essentials in life?

3. *Study your superannuation.* What has been your fund's performance? Do you have the right asset balance for risk vs return? Should you top up your super—especially before the end of the financial year? Have you checked the fees your fund is charging? When is the fund's AGM (Annual General Meeting)? As a member, maybe you should attend.

4. *Check your investments.* How are they performing? Do you have the right portfolio balance? What income are

these investments delivering? Are there some investments you should liquidate?

5. *Benchmark your investments*. Compare them to other assets in the same class. Do the research and compare their performance.

6. *Undertake a capital reserves assessment*. Are your cash reserves adequate for your plans for the next 12 months?

7. *Consider environmental changes*. Changes in the market and economy could threaten your position.

8. *Check your support structure*. You're watching your portfolio, but who's watching you?

9. *Think about new trends*. New trends or themes could affect your money or the assets you currently own.

10. *Evaluate your tax circumstances*. This must be done at least yearly.

It all starts with being honest in your evaluation of your current financial position and assessing your tolerance for risk when it comes to investment.

Starting to plan early when it comes to investing is critical. Keep building up your investments where you can each year—or even monthly if possible.

Meaningful investment planning is something you should do at least once a year with your financial planner or accountant.

TAX-PLANNING STRATEGIES

Tax is one area that can really help build your wealth if you plan properly. Here are some tax-planning strategies that should be considered prior to 30 June each year:

- *Expenses*

  Business expenses can be written off as a tax deduction and the good news is sometimes you don't have to wait to take advantage of a tax deduction. Small businesses (entities with a business turnover of less than $10 million) and medium-sized business (entities with a business turnover of between $10 million and $50 million) can claim a tax deduction for prepayments made over an advance period of up to 12 months after the end of the financial year. It's worth looking into and checking with your accountant whether you're eligible. It's especially important if the business has had a good year and you're seeking to reduce the tax burden.

- *Income deductions*

  If you've earned a little bit more than usual in the financial year and you're worried about it pushing you into a higher tax bracket, then hold onto those invoices you're about to send until the new financial year or push the pay date back. Also, if you've got some spare income, think about other things that might reduce your tax such as a donation to a tax-deductible charity. That way it's a win–win for both you and the charity. Of course, the reverse is true if your income is down one year and you're expecting a bumper year the next year. Maybe try contacting those who still owe you money and see if they can pay you in the current financial year.

(continued)

- *Home office tax deductions*

  Increasingly since COVID-19 we are working from home generating additional expenses on the home front that can be written off. One way of doing this is to claim all the additional equipment you've purchased to set up your home office. Another way is to use the ATO's 'shortcut' deduction method, which allows you to automatically claim 80 cents per hour off your tax bill for every hour you've worked from home in that financial year. That doesn't immediately sound like much, but it all adds up. The downside, of course, is if you use the shortcut method you can't claim all those other expenses, such as a portion of your phone or electricity bill to heat your house or apartment while you're working from home.

- *Tax deductions for assets*

  When COVID-19 hit and the economy needed a stimulus, there were changes to how businesses can claim an immediate tax deduction for new plant and equipment items. These applied to both smaller (under $50 million turnover) and bigger (up to $5 billion) businesses. Investors in those businesses might have received a tax benefit that improves cashflow. Check with your accountant.

- *Debtors*

  If you run a small business, are self-employed or simply run the family's finances, you should always review those who owe you money, how long the debt has been outstanding and, after contacting the debtor, whether they are likely to pay within the financial year. Remember, expenses for a business can be written off on taxes and of course the extra income can also come in handy. Sometimes when you know those funds aren't coming, that debt should be written off as a bad debt for tax and accounting purposes.

- *Superannuation contributions*

  This is another way of reducing your tax bill immediately before the end of each financial year and boosting your super balance at the same time. In this book we've already talked about how the superannuation industry is likely to be subject to future change and political interference and also unlikely to be enough to fully assist you financially in retirement, but it is a very tax-effective way to save and should be maximised.

  There are limits, of course, on the amount an individual taxpayer can deduct in concessional contributions (which includes employer contributions already made on your behalf). At the time of writing, the limit is $25000 annually. If your superannuation hasn't reached that contribution level in the financial year and you've got some spare income, top it up to claim an additional tax deduction.

  There is one other top-up to your superannuation you should consider, if you're eligible. Recent changes to the law mean if your super balance is below $500000 and in previous years you didn't meet the $25000 concessional cap, you can make extra contributions. Check the details with your accountant or the ATO.

- *Tax rates and rulings*

  Every year there are changes to tax rates and tax rulings that you should be aware of. It's a conversation you should regularly have with your accountant. Many taxpayers, particularly high-net-worth taxpayers in Australia, operate under a family trust structure to minimise tax. Recent ATO changes have meant they have changed the way they tax trusts, when it comes to trust distributions, sometimes stretching all the way back to distributions made in 2015. The reasoning behind these

  (continued)

changes was fair—to stop bogus distributions being made to family members—but the implications for some trust structures have been significant. Is it still okay to distribute to children or grandparents? It is worth being aware of these changes as the ATO is watching family distributions very carefully.

In another change, if you operate what the ATO calls a 'base rate entity'—that is, a company with a turnover of under $50 million and earning less than 80 per cent of its income from passive sources—the good news is your tax rate has been reduced to 25 per cent. That can have some implications for investors in those companies because it can affect the rate at which they can frank dividends to those shareholders.

- *Business structure*

  Take some time to consider with your accountant whether you have the most efficient business structure. Changing the structure should not trigger any capital gains tax issues and there are often tax concessions available to help you achieve that process.

  When it comes to end-of-financial-year tax considerations, just remember that circumstances may have changed since you first established your business structure, which may have been many years ago. Re-evaluate our own personal and business circumstances and review them with a forensic eye, with the help of your financial adviser or accountant. The end of a financial year is the ideal time to reflect and plan.

  The perfect time to start a new business structure is on the first day of a new financial year. This process needs to be done carefully, though, to ensure the business achieves the best tax and operational structure.

Ten tactics for planning your life and business

In addition to tax planning, life planning should also be done at least once a year. It should not be considered less important than your financial or tax review, but as you know by now, I'm all about embracing a holistic approach to achieving your next set of goals.

Here's a list of 10 critical pre-match questions you should ask in your business life and in your personal life, at least at the beginning of each year. These are not New Year's resolutions, which we know few people stick to, but should become the norm each year.

1. How's your physical shape and health? There's no point in embarking on something new or a new strategy if you won't last the distance. Being match fit is more than just having the cash available to embark on a new project—it's how committed you are to the work ahead of you.

2. When did you last have a break? Is there a holiday planned with family or friends? Are you at risk of burnout?

3. What's your key purpose for enhancing your life financially? Please think clearly on your *why* when answering this question.

4. What's your plan for business, investment and achieving the things you desire—material or not?

5. Have you set out some well-written and clear short- and long-term goals?

6. What are your strengths, weaknesses, opportunities and threats (SWOT), both now and in the future?

7. What's your personal reward if you accomplish your goals in the next 12 months? Is there a special treat, obviously within your budget, that you can justify giving yourself for working so hard?

8. Have you established the proper legal structures to enhance taxation concessions and deductions and protect your assets and family wealth?

9. Do you have a great accountant as well as a person who understands your business and you?

10. Do you have a great finance and banking partner who also understands your growth plans and your requirements now and into the foreseeable future?

This all sounds time-consuming, I know — but as I've emphasised repeatedly in this book, planning is the key to intelligent leverage.

LET'S REFLECT...

- Change doesn't happen without planning—and planning should be done weekly, monthly and yearly.

- There are a number of important things you should evaluate at least yearly, with tax and your investment portfolio being key priorities.

- Part of planning is having goals and revisiting them regularly.

- Be honest in your evaluation of your current financial position and assess your tolerance for risk when it comes to investment.

- Good tax-planning strategies are important for helping build your wealth.

- Don't be afraid to also evaluate yourself. What are your strengths and weaknesses and how can you improve?

PART III: KEY TAKEAWAYS

- Stay positive, be grateful and appreciate those around you.

- How you use your time is critical. Create tools and methods that will allow you to grab an hour each day to think and plan.

- Constantly evaluate your progress. When it comes to investments you should do this at least monthly and for yourself weekly.

- Create the right networks around you: support, guidance and encouragement are essential.

- Remember the importance of planning.

POSTSCRIPT

Let me remind you of something powerful. Tomorrow represents a brand-new day — the great refresher — and each day offers the same opportunity. The future is ahead of you so think of ways to increase your effectiveness and achieve your goals, both personal and financial.

Think of tomorrow as a fresh new page on which to write the story of your life. The past is important, as we all learn from our mistakes and gather strength from our progress, but the past is gone and there is nothing we can do to change that.

Equally, it's important you don't concern yourself with the opportunities you may have missed. Opportunities abound and if we just use one hour each day to plan, analyse and evaluate our goals then we've bought an extra 365 hours a year to put to good use.

Whether your employer pays for this 'extra' hour during your lunch break or you do it after hours isn't important — either way, it will help make you a happier and more productive worker. Of course, if you're doing it during business hours and you're self-employed then you're investing in your business.

A human life is really a collection of experiences (both positive and negative) spread over hours, days and months. We need to take control of time and use any extra time we have to determine what outcomes we can achieve.

We can dramatically increase our effective mission in life by intelligently leveraging the tools we have at our disposal.

Use that extra hour to make a new contact and build your network. If you do, you might have more than 1000 people in your network within a decade—although I suggest never overloading your life with people.

Then there are the overflow effects of a positive mental attitude in your home life and with friends.

Each morning when we start our day, whether we realise it or not, our attitude determines how we are viewed. We are responsible for our outlook.

I remember some years ago when a man and his wife bought a home across the street from my home in Melbourne. They had moved down from Queensland and planned to retire here. I went to meet them when they first moved in so I could introduce myself and welcome them to the neighbourhood. Several months later, I was shocked to see them packing up again. I asked the husband why they were leaving.

He said his wife was hating being in Melbourne as she'd made no friends and wasn't participating in any community activities, like she did in Queensland.

I asked if she'd reached out to anyone. It turns out she'd spoken to one local person and told her she was interested in participating in community activities and she'd been waiting at home for that person to come to her for offers to join groups. I was amazed at her passive attitude.

We can all make a difference; we just need to alter our outlook.

Learning any new habit takes time, but once it becomes a habit, we can change the way we live our lives forever—with gratitude and without having too many expectations.

Taking life's opportunities

In 1994, I was running along a Sydney beach. I used to do a lot of competitive running and competed in some professional races such as the famous Stawell Gift Carnival in Victoria as a young adult. To my amazement running the other way on the same beach for a morning jog was the great English sprinter Linford Christie.

At the time, Linford was the reigning Olympic gold medal champion, having won the 100-metre sprint at the 1992 Barcelona Olympics. I was taken aback by the man's physique. I had never seen a fitter person in my life, and he was mesmerising. In fact no-one on the beach could take their eyes off him. When I acknowledged him, Linford kindly stopped and we chatted.

I asked him about his secret to success. I was expecting his answer to be something deep and meaningful to do with his training methods or his technique during the race. Instead he said to me that 90 per cent of his training was, in-fact, long, intense sessions of stretching before the race, and keeping all his muscles loose and ready to perform. His comments hit me again when I put them in the context of life, business success or achieving personal investment goals. In other words, what he was saying, was it is all about the preparation. It's the little things, like doing enough stretching before a run. And it all comes down to both planning and preparation before execution.

We all are fortunate to meet amazing people in our lives. An exceptional recollection of mine was meeting Buzz Aldrin, the second man to step on the moon after Neil Armstrong and the pilot of the 1969 *Apollo 11* mission. It was at a party in Austin, Texas, where I'd flown to for some meetings. To tell you the truth, I was jetlagged and didn't want to go to the party.

I'd arrived at the airport in Austin at about 10 pm and was heading to my house I'd kept in Texas for business meetings. I arrived at my front door exhausted. Even at 10.30 pm the air felt like 38 degrees Celsius, so stepping into a refrigerated air-conditioned house offered some reprieve.

I'd barely been home a few minutes when the phone went ballistic. A retired businessman I knew called Charlie Alexander was having one of his famous big parties with some local folk from Austin and Horseshow Bay. These partygoers were yelling and screaming down the phone saying, 'When are you coming? We need to see the Aussie man over here at this party'.

I reluctantly threw my case into one of the spare rooms, had one Red Bull to get me going and proceeded to the party. When I arrived, the door was wide open, and everyone seemed to be very, very lightly dressed, it being August, the hottest month that you could possibly pick to go anywhere in the United States and in particular, Texas!

I walked through the party and all I could hear was my name being called from different corners of the room. It was 'Paul, Paul come over here'. I wasn't sure which direction to take, so decided to head up the house's monstrous staircase to where the balcony was situated in the massive 75- to 80-square house overlooking Lake Lyndon B Johnson.

I was then greeted by some good friends of mine, some important business partners I had spent a lot of time with over the previous decade, including Charlie. Charlie said I had to meet some people (but didn't tell me who he was introducing me to).

Charlie took me out to the balcony where three men were drinking cognac from fishbowl glasses. One or two of them were also smoking big cigars and they seemed to be in their advancing years. The first man ran a big excavating business in Texas, which was impressive enough given the size of the construction industry in the United States at that time. The second man was a banker whose son I knew. The last gentleman I was introduced to was called Buzz. I didn't quite recognise him, although the name should certainly have been a giveaway. The four gentlemen paused and stared at me and then started laughing. The penny dropped.

The words fell from my mouth: 'It's incredible to meet you, Buzz. I've flown from the other side of the world to meet you'. My mind was buzzing about business and life and I was exhausted and jetlagged. Then I looked up, and to my surprise right behind Buzz's right shoulder was a full moon. It was total synchronicity. In fact, the moon was as big as a basketball in the sky that night.

This sight of the man who had stepped on the moon with the actual moon as his backdrop was overpowering. The adrenaline kicked in and the tiredness and weirdness subsided. It was a life-changing moment to shake the hand of Buzz Aldrin, who had been to the earth's only natural satellite, and we talked for a long time about how he overcame his challenges to get to the moon.

There are moments like this, my grandfather reminded me as a child, when the most important thing is to present yourself well. What's equally important are the words that come from your mouth when you meet someone for the first time. It's about creating a memorable first impression of yourself.

I remember Buzz put his arm on my shoulder at one point and he said: 'Son, I'm so glad that you're here. We've all been waiting for you and waiting for your stories about Australia and what they get up to over there'. It turns out Buzz was most interested in Australia's reputation for deadly animals, from sharks and crocodiles to snakes. He also loved kangaroos. If you try, you will always find something in common to engage with others, no matter how famous they are in life.

That night I probably got more out of Buzz Aldrin than he got out of me, but to this day that meeting reminds me to take chances in life, to go to that meeting (even when you're jetlagged) and to try to engage. You never know who you'll meet.

One thing my great grandfather used to say to motivate me and make me contemplate was to think about meeting the man 'that you could have been'—meaning, don't have regrets.

Leveraging intelligently

I hope one of the key takeaways from this book on intelligent leverage is to be very conscious of time, be very mindful of the people around you, never give up on your goals and think about the future—because that's where you'll be living. Always think big, but set realistic goals and plans.

In the dog-eat-dog nature of competitive business, the conservativism of financial institutions and the general ineffectiveness of governments, envious people will always try to keep you down, to force you to think small, because that's what they want.

Some of the people who advise you, lend you money or seek to become your business partners will gladly take your money and hope you'll sit there being humble and accept their directions.

The bad news is the deck is generally stacked against you, especially given the ongoing cost-of-living pressures and the ever-growing requirements for financial success. That means you can't afford to think small. You have to build a trusted team around you to collaborate with because it will be too hard to do it on your own, and you need to dream.

The good news is there is a way to navigate through and hit your financial and life aspirations.

Life is a privilege so enjoy leveraging it every day you can— intelligently of course.

LET'S ACT

- *Weekly work assessment:* You planned your week and then you went to work—the key is to measure your progress. Use this template every week to score your progress and keep track of your mindset so that weeks, months or even years down the track you can physically measure how you are tracking. All too often people leave this task to the recesses of their minds but soon enough the weeks will start to blend together, and momentum will be lost. Measure, Measure, Measure, Assess and Measure! Follow the QR code to download your weekly work assessment template.

- *Weekly health assessment:* Taking action and ticking items off your to-do list is one thing, but it all falls apart if you aren't keeping check of your own health and wellbeing. For that reason, I have included my health assessment template for you to download and use. Measure your health and wellbeing progress the same way you measure your work. When it comes to successful outcomes, you'll be surprised how closely the two areas are related. Follow the QR code to download your weekly health assessment template.

ACKNOWLEDGEMENTS

I would not have achieved half of what I've done in life without a lot of support and mentoring.

I'd particularly like to pay tribute to my CEO at Lendlease, Stuart Hornery, who had faith in me by letting me take on the company's fund management business.

I've been fortunate to meet with well-known personal development trainer and keynote speaker Brian Tracy on a few occasions and I follow his training methods, which I adopted 30 years ago. Those methods really reinforced to me the importance of sales, marketing, self-esteem and promoting self-image.

Given my funds management background, I've also been able to meet with Ray Dalio from Bridgewater, which has changed the way I operate today, not just from an investment perspective, but also in how I interact with my colleagues and the people in my life.

My family has been a big part of my success. In particular, thanks to my mother Margaret who's been so loving and outstanding. My two siblings, Mark and Amanda, have always been there and I'm so pleased to say we've always been particularly close.

My partner Sally, an experienced lawyer who works for me in the firm, has been the most loyal and giving person I've met in my life.

The most enjoyable moments I have on the weekends today are certainly with my son Harrison, who is now 18 years of age. He has always been the joy of my life.